OPPOSING VIEWPOINTS® SERIES

Online Pornography

Other Books of Related Interest:

Opposing Viewpoints Series

Censorship

At Issue Series

Policing the Internet

Current Controversies Series

The Global Impact of Social Media

"Congress shall make no law . . . abridging the freedom of speech, or of the press."

First Amendment to the US Constitution

The basic foundation of our democracy is the First Amendment guarantee of freedom of expression. The Opposing Viewpoints series is dedicated to the concept of this basic freedom and the idea that it is more important to practice it than to enshrine it.

OPPOSING VIEWPOINTS® SERIES

Online Pornography

David E. Nelson, Book Editor

GREENHAVEN PRESS
A part of Gale, Cengage Learning

GALE
CENGAGE Learning·

Detroit • New York • San Francisco • New Haven, Conn • Waterville, Maine • London

Elizabeth Des Chenes, *Director, Publishing Solutions*

© 2012 Greenhaven Press, a part of Gale, Cengage Learning.

For more information, contact:
Greenhaven Press
27500 Drake Rd.
Farmington Hills, MI 48331-3535
Or you can visit our Internet site at gale.cengage.com

For product information and technology assistance, contact us at

Gale Customer Support, 1-800-877-4253
For permission to use material from this text or product, submit all requests online at www.cengage.com/permissions

Further permissions questions can be emailed to permissionrequest@cengage.com

Articles in Greenhaven Press anthologies are often edited for length to meet page requirements. In addition, original titles of these works are changed to clearly present the main thesis and to explicitly indicate the author's opinion. Every effort is made to ensure that Greenhaven Press accurately reflects the original intent of the authors. Every effort has been made to trace the owners of copyrighted material.

Cover Image copyright © Mike Kemp/Tetra Images/Alamy.

LIBRARY OF CONGRESS CATALOGING-IN-PUBLICATION DATA

Online pornography / David E. Nelson, book editor.
   p. cm. -- (Opposing viewpoints)
   Includes bibliographical references and index.
   ISBN 978-0-7377-5905-1 (hbk.) -- ISBN 978-0-7377-5906-8 (pbk.)
   1. Internet pornography. 2. Children and pornography. 3. Internet--Law and legislation. I. Nelson, David Erik.
   HQ471.O552 2012
   363.4'702854678--dc23

                                            2012005718

Contents

Chapter 3: Is Online Pornography a Special Threat to Minors?

Chapter 4: Can Online Pornography Be Regulated?

Why Consider Opposing Viewpoints?

> *"The only way in which a human being can make some approach to knowing the whole of a subject is by hearing what can be said about it by persons of every variety of opinion and studying all modes in which it can be looked at by every character of mind. No wise man ever acquired his wisdom in any mode but this."*
>
> *John Stuart Mill*

In our media-intensive culture it is not difficult to find differing opinions. Thousands of newspapers and magazines and dozens of radio and television talk shows resound with differing points of view. The difficulty lies in deciding which opinion to agree with and which "experts" seem the most credible. The more inundated we become with differing opinions and claims, the more essential it is to hone critical reading and thinking skills to evaluate these ideas. Opposing Viewpoints books address this problem directly by presenting stimulating debates that can be used to enhance and teach these skills. The varied opinions contained in each book examine many different aspects of a single issue. While examining these conveniently edited opposing views, readers can develop critical thinking skills such as the ability to compare and contrast authors' credibility, facts, argumentation styles, use of persuasive techniques, and other stylistic tools. In short, the Opposing Viewpoints Series is an ideal way to attain the higher-level thinking and reading skills so essential in a culture of diverse and contradictory opinions.

In addition to providing a tool for critical thinking, Opposing Viewpoints books challenge readers to question their own strongly held opinions and assumptions. Most people form their opinions on the basis of upbringing, peer pressure, and personal, cultural, or professional bias. By reading carefully balanced opposing views, readers must directly confront new ideas as well as the opinions of those with whom they disagree. This is not to argue simplistically that everyone who reads opposing views will—or should—change his or her opinion. Instead, the series enhances readers' understanding of their own views by encouraging confrontation with opposing ideas. Careful examination of others' views can lead to the readers' understanding of the logical inconsistencies in their own opinions, perspective on why they hold an opinion, and the consideration of the possibility that their opinion requires further evaluation.

Evaluating Other Opinions

To ensure that this type of examination occurs, Opposing Viewpoints books present all types of opinions. Prominent spokespeople on different sides of each issue as well as well-known professionals from many disciplines challenge the reader. An additional goal of the series is to provide a forum for other, less known, or even unpopular viewpoints. The opinion of an ordinary person who has had to make the decision to cut off life support from a terminally ill relative, for example, may be just as valuable and provide just as much insight as a medical ethicist's professional opinion. The editors have two additional purposes in including these less known views. One, the editors encourage readers to respect others' opinions—even when not enhanced by professional credibility. It is only by reading or listening to and objectively evaluating others' ideas that one can determine whether they are worthy of consideration. Two, the inclusion of such viewpoints encourages the important critical thinking skill of objectively evaluating an author's credentials and bias. This evaluation will illuminate an author's reasons for taking a particular stance on an issue and will aid in readers' evaluation of the author's ideas.

It is our hope that these books will give readers a deeper understanding of the issues debated and an appreciation of the complexity of even seemingly simple issues when good and honest people disagree. This awareness is particularly important in a democratic society such as ours in which people enter into public debate to determine the common good. Those with whom one disagrees should not be regarded as enemies but rather as people whose views deserve careful examination and may shed light on one's own.

Thomas Jefferson once said that "difference of opinion leads to inquiry, and inquiry to truth." Jefferson, a broadly educated man, argued that "if a nation expects to be ignorant and free ... it expects what never was and never will be." As individuals and as a nation, it is imperative that we consider the opinions of others and examine them with skill and discernment. The Opposing Viewpoints series is intended to help readers achieve this goal.

David L. Bender and Bruno Leone,
Founders

Introduction

> *"I shall not . . . attempt further to define the kinds of material I understand to be embraced within that shorthand description [hard-core pornography]; and perhaps I could never succeed in intelligibly doing so. But I know it when I see it."*
>
> —US Supreme Court
> Justice Potter Stewart,
> *in* Jacobellis v. Ohio, *1964.*

Obscenity has been banned by US federal law since at least the mid-1800s. Early on, this ban included a wide range of material, from pornographic drawings and erotic writings to scientific pamphlets on abortion and practical advice on birth control. Over the course of decades, an increasing amount of so-called obscene material has been accepted as important speech protected under the First Amendment. Today, the fuzzy divide between illegal obscenity and protected speech is determined by the three-part "Miller test," so called because it was a result of the 1974 US Supreme Court case *Miller v. California*. According to the Miller test, material can only be deemed obscene if:

1. "the average person, applying contemporary community standards," would find that the entire work only appeals to a morbid, degrading, and unhealthy interest in sex, as opposed to simply a candid interest in sex;

2. the work offensively depicts *actual* sexual acts; and

3. the entire work "lacks serious literary, artistic, political, or scientific value."

Around the time of the *Miller* decision the first feature-length pornographic films were being produced in the United

States. Although these early films were shot in many locations, the industry quickly settled in Los Angeles's San Fernando Valley, whose close proximity to Hollywood production lots offered a ready supply of professional-quality film equipment, trained technical workers, and starry-eyed performers. Owing to the permissive culture of Southern California, these San Fernando–based adult film producers also enjoyed protection under the three-part Miller test for obscenity: Their works were of arguable artistic value, and they certainly depicted sex acts, but they were being produced and largely marketed in a community where the standards were accepting of such productions. In other words, they failed to qualify as obscenity able to be prohibited under the first condition of the Miller test, thereby establishing California pornography as constitutionally protected speech. The so-called "Porn Valley" adult industry puttered along, only occasionally attracting prosecution, and rarely suffering any real legal setbacks.

The dawning of the Internet age should have doomed Porn Valley. The first part of the Miller test speaks to contemporary community standards without defining what a "community" is. Throughout the first two decades after *Miller*, the courts interpreted this to mean the immediate geographical community: The bulk of successful obscenity prosecutions were targeted at shops and adult movie theaters, or distributors shipping magazines and movies into conservative communities across state lines. The producers themselves stayed safely ensconced in Porn Valley, where their business model was grudgingly accepted. But as pornographers moved to the Internet, they shifted from being simple "filmmakers" to "web masters," distributing their own materials and reaping a larger slice of the profits. Broadband Internet easily ferried videos from permissive Porn Valley to the conservative Bible Belt, where the community's standards were very different. It seemed like only a matter of time before obscenity charges would rain down, forcing San Fernando pornographers to travel all over the country defending themselves in court.

But that day of reckoning never came. Throughout the Bill Clinton administration of the 1990s, obscenity prosecutions were deemphasized at the Department of Justice. Following the election of the far more conservative George W. Bush, legal scholars and industry watchers once again waited for a deluge of obscenity charges. But the new Bush administration, concerned with terror attacks, airport security, and two foreign wars, proved unwilling to send the Department of Justice after pornographers. Provided a film or picture didn't depict an underage performer, a person being coerced, or harm coming to a child or animal, it was highly unlikely that federal agents would come knocking at producers' doors.

All told, the new Internet porn industry had more than fifteen years in which to grow, limited only by market demand. That demand was for ever kinkier and more extreme content, often tailored to tastes and fetishes that, just a few years earlier, were largely unknown to most Americans. By the middle of the first decade of the twenty-first century, some porn actors and actresses had become household names, and sexual kinks that were once punishable with prison time had become wry punch lines in prime-time sitcoms.

Then, in 2008, Porn Valley's Paul F. Little—who produced, directed, and performed in extremely degrading gonzo pornography under the name "Max Hardcore"—was raided, indicted, and convicted on five obscenity counts. This was a straight obscenity prosecution: The Department of Justice never claimed that any performer was under the age of eighteen or had been coerced, that an animal had been harmed, or that Hardcore's final product was ever accessed by any child. The jury found that the material *itself* was so patently offensive and without merit that it qualified as obscenity. Little ultimately served almost four years in prison. Porn Valley had every reason to be surprised: Little had faced virtually the same charges a decade earlier, in 1998, but no jury would convict him.

While many left-leaning pundits and civil libertarians were quick to write columns decrying this verdict as a chilling attack on free expression, it turned out that many of these defenders had never watched any of the videos they were defending. Susannah Breslin—a longtime porn industry documentarian—remains impartial about Hardcore's conviction, but not about his work, which she *has* watched. In an article on True/Slant.com Breslin said:

> Hardcore's movies are not for the faint of heart. They are targeted at a demographic one would perhaps rather not dwell upon the existence of for any length of time. They are less 'movies' and more political demonstrations: of power, of violence, of one man's seeming frustration with the opposite sex. . . . Max's movies aren't shocking—not most significantly. They are *sad*. Everyone suffers. No one is happy. If joy is located at one end of the spectrum, this is where its opposite resides.

Any civil liberties activist will be quick to point out that no one has trouble protecting free speech when it's saying something they like; the test of the First Amendment is in protecting unpopular and unpleasant speech. The case of Max Hardcore caused many to ask whether what he does can be described, in any meaningful way, as "speech," or is it simply a demonstration of one man's violent frustration with women. While the courts ruled in Max Hardcore's case that such expression was not worthy of protection, the larger issue of the constitutional rights of pornographers continue to be debated.

The contributors to *Opposing Viewpoints: Online Pornography* explore the full spectrum of pornography, including its many effects—often unpredictable and seemingly illogical—on individuals and society. They do so in the following chapters: What Is the Impact of Online Pornography on Society?, What Is the Impact of Online Pornography on Individuals?, Is Online Pornography a Special Threat to Minors?, and Can Online Pornography Be Regulated?

OPPOSING
VIEWPOINTS®
SERIES

CHAPTER 1

What Is the Impact of Online Pornography on Society?

Chapter Preface

Since the mid-1800s, the US federal government has enacted a variety of laws meant to curb or eliminate the production and distribution of pornography. Most notable of these was Anthony Comstock's 1873 Act for the Suppression of Trade in, and Circulation of, Obscene Literature and Articles of Immoral Use, commonly called the Comstock Act. This made it a federal crime, punishable by hard labor:

> to sell, or to lend, or to give away, or in any manner to exhibit, or . . . publish or offer to publish in any manner, or . . . have in his possession, for any such purpose or purposes, an obscene book, pamphlet, paper, writing, advertisement, circular, print, picture, drawing or other representation, figure, or image.

Although the Comstock Act has been modified through court decision and legislation, this federal law has never been repealed.

What has likewise remained unchanged is Comstock's basic assumption that "obscene" material, whatever it may be, is in some way dangerous and must be destroyed in order to protect civilization.

On the one hand, almost anyone can produce an anecdote about how damaging pornography can be, ranging from various serial killers' purported, or admitted, fascination with pornography, to a coworker's son running up a $1,000 credit card bill on Internet porn sites. Advice columns and talk shows seem to suffer no lack of marriages destroyed by "porn addiction." Pundits across the political spectrum decry the "porning" of America and the inevitable destruction of faith, family, home, and country. In their defense, plenty of experimental research does tend to indicate that pornography *should* have a negative impact on society: Controlled studies have consistently found that as test subjects, especially men, view sexualized images or greater amounts of a person's body, they increasingly see others as "objects" instead of people.

In light of the many small studies confirming the immediate objectification that results from viewing pornography, it would seem elementary that these negative attitudes must almost certainly be carried out into the world, where they'll be magnified and have a negative impact on how men and women interact in the bedroom, the workplace, and beyond. But large-scale research into the long-term cultural ramifications of increased exposure to pornography has been inconclusive. No reliable, longitudinal study—of either specific groups (such as Canadian customs agents, who are exposed to a large amount of very offensive pornographic material as part of their work) or general mixed populations—has demonstrated any consistent consequence, positive or negative, associated with the viewing of pornography. In fact, a 2010 report from the US Department of Justice's Bureau of Justice Statistics, based on its annual National Crime Victimization Survey, found that over the last decade "serious violent crime," including rape/sexual assault, robbery, and aggravated assault, dropped 39 percent, while the incidences of rape alone fell by 57 percent, even as reporting on violent crime remained steady. For 2008–2009, serious violent crime only dipped 7.7 percent, but rapes still fell by almost 39 percent.

Even as online pornography has brought an ever-increasing number of sexual images—generally agreed to be more graphic and extreme with each passing year—into American homes, violent crime has dropped significantly, with sexual assaults more than halved. This seems to fly in the face of both reason and experimental research.

The authors in the following chapter explore many facets of the impact online pornography has on American culture. While they offer no consensus—and in fact can hardly agree on even basic points—their arguments offer a solid base from which to examine this phenomenon.

> "Americans now spend ... around $10 billion a year on adult entertainment ... as much as they spend attending professional sporting events, buying music or going out to the movies."

Pornography Is a Major Industry

Rebecca Leung

In the following viewpoint, Rebecca Leung argues that, by virtue of its early adoption of online technology, pornography has grown into a $10 billion dollar American industry. Porn's substantial profit margins and high demand have subsequently paved the way for pornographers to join forces with established industries, from luxury hotel chains to media empires. Leung has worked as a producer for CBS News, ABC News, and CNET News, as well as an editor for TheStreet.com. She now teaches at Columbia University's Graduate School of Journalism.

As you read, consider the following questions:

1. According to Bill Lyon, how many Californians are employed by the porn industry, and how much does the porn industry in California pay in taxes each year?

2. Name two technologies that were pioneered by online pornographers.

3. How does the US Supreme Court define obscenity? What kind of pornography is absolutely illegal?

Selling sex is one of the oldest businesses in the world, and right now, business has never been better.

One of the biggest cultural changes in the United States over the past 25 years has been the widespread acceptance of sexually explicit material—pornography.

In the space of a generation, a product that once was available in the back alleys of big cities has gone corporate, delivered now directly into homes and hotel rooms by some of the biggest companies in the United States.

It is estimated that Americans now spend somewhere around $10 billion a year on adult entertainment, which is as much as they spend attending professional sporting events, buying music or going out to the movies.

From Underground to Big Business

Consumer demand is so strong that it has seduced some of America's biggest brand names, and companies like General Motors, Marriott and Time Warner are now making millions selling erotica to America. Last November [*60 Minutes*] correspondent Steve Kroft reported on this billion-dollar industry.

The best place to see it is at the industry's annual convention in Las Vegas, where more than 200 adult entertainment companies gather under one roof to network, schmooze and show off their latest wares.

Presiding over it all is Paul Fishbein, the founder and president of *Adult Video News*, the industry's trade publication, which sponsors the expo.

Who's out there? "Manufacturers of adult products, distributors, suppliers, retail store owners, wholesalers, distributors, cable TV buyers, foreign buyers," says Fishbein. "They're all here to do business, and then you have the fans."

The fans came from all over the country, stood in line for hours, and paid $40 to get into what was essentially an X-rated trade show. From appearances, you might find the same crowd at the boat show.

According to Fishbein, there are well over 800 million rentals of adult videotapes and DVDs in video stores across the country. "And I don't think that it's 800 guys renting a million tapes each," he says.

Suffice it to say, there was something available for every sexual demographic—even material aimed at the *60 Minutes* crowd.

A Mature Industry

In Fishbein's words, all of this is performed and produced by consenting adults, for the use of consenting adults in the privacy of their own homes. The industry also has its own major studios.

"Here you have two of the leading companies in the business, VCA and Vivid," says Fishbein. "They're known for the biggest-budget top movies in the industry, along with Wicked Pictures."

The industry also has its own major stars, like Jenna Jameson, a teen beauty queen, turned showgirl, turned porn actress. With the approval of her family, she reportedly earned more than a million dollars last year [2006] performing sex for money.

"The way I look at it is, this is kind of an art to me. I'm performing. I'm not doing it for the gratification of another man," says Jameson. "I'm doing it because this is my job and I'm entertaining the masses. So it's just like being Julia Roberts, but just a little bit further, one step further."

The porn world now has all the trappings of a legitimate industry with considerable economic clout. Besides its own convention and trade publication, it holds marketing and legal seminars. It even has its own lobbyist.

"It employs in excess of 12,000 people in California. And in California alone, we pay over $36 million in taxes every year. So it's a very sizeable industry," says Bill Lyon, a former lobbyist for the defense industry.

When *60 Minutes* first spoke to Lyon, he was running the Free Speech Coalition, a trade organization that represents 900 companies in the porn business.

"I was rather shocked to find that these are pretty bright businesspeople who are in it to make a profit. And that is what it's about," says Lyon.

What kind of reaction does he expect to get when he tells legislators all over the country that he's a lobbyist for the adult entertainment business?

"Initially, I think there's a degree of shock. But when you explain to them the size and the scope of the business, they realize, as all politicians do, that it's votes and money that we're talking about," adds Lyon, who says there are reputable companies traded on the New York Stock Exchange that are involved in the business. "Corporations are in business to make money. This is an extremely large business and there's a great opportunity for profits in it."

Porn Partners with Established Industries

In 2002, Comcast, the nation's largest cable company, pulled in $50 million from adult programming. All the nation's top cable operators, from Time Warner to Cablevision, distribute sexually explicit material to their subscribers. But you won't read about it in their annual reports. Same with satellite providers like EchoStar and DirecTV, which is owned by Hughes [Electronics], a subsidiary of General Motors.

How much does DirecTV make off of adult product?

"They don't break the number out. But I would guess they'd probably get a couple hundred million, maybe as much as $500 million, off of adult entertainment, in a broad sense," says Dennis McAlpine, a partner in McAlpine Associates, who has tracked the entertainment industry for over two decades. "I would think it's probably more than what their overall profit is. The other areas are losing money. That's making money."

Then there are the big hotel chains: Hilton, Marriott, Hyatt, Sheraton and Holiday Inn, which all offer adult films on in-room, pay-per-view television systems. And they are purchased by a whopping 50 percent of their guests, accounting for nearly 70 percent of their in-room profits. One hotel owner said, "We have to have it. Our guests demand it."

One of the largest owners and programmers of in-room, pay-per-view is Liberty Media, a publicly traded company run by media mogul John Malone, one of the most powerful people in the communications industry.

McAlpine says that adult entertainment has become a critical part of the entertainment business: "Adult is a major factor in determining the profits of a cable system, an in-house hotel system, a satellite system. It's a big profit contributor."

So how do these corporations get involved in it?

"I think that they get involved in it because of the profit margins that are involved. One of the things about pornography that's consistently true across the board is that because there's a social stigma still attached to it, you can charge a premium for these materials. And because you can charge a premium for it, the profit margin is higher. So, it makes pure economic sense," says Fred Lane, a lawyer and author of a book called *Obscene Profits: The Entrepreneurs of Pornography in the Cyber Age.*

Major Corporations Are Attracted to Porn's Big Profit Margins

The epicenter of the porn industry is Chatsworth, Calif., a quiet suburb north of Los Angeles. It is indistinguishable from

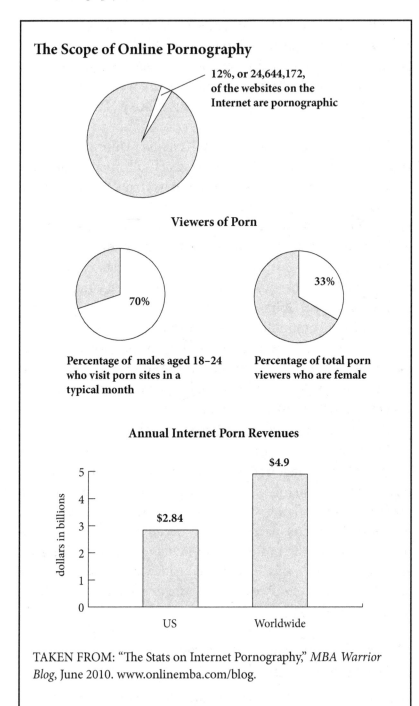

The Scope of Online Pornography

12%, or 24,644,172, of the websites on the Internet are pornographic

Viewers of Porn

70%

Percentage of males aged 18–24 who visit porn sites in a typical month

33%

Percentage of total porn viewers who are female

Annual Internet Porn Revenues

$2.84 — US

$4.9 — Worldwide

dollars in billions

TAKEN FROM: "The Stats on Internet Pornography," *MBA Warrior Blog*, June 2010. www.onlinemba.com/blog.

the other middle-class communities that sprawl across the San Fernando Valley, except for one thing.

Tucked among the defense contractors and aerospace companies are dozens and dozens of adult film companies like Vivid [Entertainment], the porn industry equivalent of Paramount [Pictures] or Universal [Pictures]. It makes adult films, distributes them on video, DVD, and then sells them to hotels, cable companies and over the Internet.

Bill Asher, Vivid's president, says these films are relatively inexpensive to produce, and Vivid has had double-digit growth every year for the past five years. Last year, he says, consumers spent a billion dollars on Vivid products.

"We know that when we were selling the content to certain satellite companies, they did an analysis, and we were the most profitable channel they had for the distributor," says Asher. "I would say it [cable systems] is the most profitable channel. . . . The industry is big business now. It's mainstream. It's really no different than what *Playboy* was 30 years ago, 20 years ago."

Asher, who graduated from Dartmouth and has an MBA, used to work at *Playboy* as a financial analyst.

"It's an issue of distribution. When customers can get to adult content, generally, they buy it. They enjoy it. The question was, 'Would mainstream companies distribute it?' Now, *Playboy* and *Penthouse* for 30 years have enjoyed the same distribution as other magazines. Adult movies really didn't have that up until recently," adds Asher.

"And what happened was, as companies like Vivid came around, and made everyone more comfortable with adult product, mainstream companies said, 'OK, we'll be willing to distribute it. We would like to join in the benefit—the financial benefit of distributing it.'"

Asher says it wasn't a hard sell. All he had to do was show and provide an upscale product on the polite side of the pornographic spectrum. "We strive to have good sets, good plots, attractive people. People who can hopefully speak and act. Everything that you would expect to see in a mainstream movie," says Asher.

60 Minutes was hoping that at least one big mainstream corporation would talk to us about its involvement in adult entertainment. But no one did. A few gave us statements saying essentially their companies provide a whole range of entertainment choices, plus the ability to block them out, and such choices should be left to the customer.

"When *60 Minutes* comes to your door asking about adult content, and you're a major corporation, my advice to you would be: 'Don't open the door,'" says Asher. "What possible victory could come out of it for them? They are offering content, the customers are buying the content, everyone is happy."

Pornography Drives Technological Development and Adoption

Adult entertainment is so lucrative and profitable that it's become part of the mainstream culture—readily available, easily accessible, and all but impossible to legislate away.

How did it happen? It began 25 years ago with a brand-new household appliance: the video cassette recorder.

"The first thing that a lot of people did when they got their VCR was rent or purchase an adult movie. *Deep Throat. The Devil in Miss Jones. Behind the Green Door. Debbie Does Dallas.* That's what they asked for," says Fishbein, who publishes *Adult Video News*, the porn industry's trade magazine.

"Most people had never seen an adult movie, because they had to go out in public, to a theater, to see it. I mean, sex is a very private thing. So, now that you can watch it in the privacy of your own home, nobody has to know. And I think that's what drove the VCR. And I think, to a degree, it's what drove a lot of people to get on the Internet."

In fact, pornography has helped drive early sales and the development of most new entertainment technologies for the past 25 years—providing software for the latest gadgets, and a reason to buy them. And usually the first people who do are affluent young men who like porn.

Type the word "sex" into an Internet search engine like Google and you will get 180 million hits. For years, adult sites were the only ones to turn a profit. They have pioneered and helped to develop numerous technological breakthroughs from online payment methods to streaming video.

Lane wrote a book about this unofficial, commercial partnership between technology and the adult entertainment industry. He believes it has had a tremendous impact on American values, popular culture, and the government's ability to regulate pornography.

"The way I like to put it is that we went from 1,000 adult movie theaters in less than 10 years to 80 million adult movie theaters. And that basically is what happened with the VCR," says Lane.

"The computer now, in terms of its penetration into American households—the last figure I saw was somewhere on the order of 70–80 million households, out of the 100 million in this country. So again, we've got enormous potential for people to look at things in the privacy of their home."

Pornography Has Become Mainstream

Has it become more difficult in the United States to win an obscenity prosecution?

Absolutely, says Lane. "And as adult materials have found their way into different communities by different means, whether it's by cable television, or it's by hotel chains, people have grown increasingly comfortable with adult materials. And there seems to me to be, I think, a growing sense that what people do in the privacy of their own homes is their business."

Porn is so accessible now that it's working its way into the subtext of American culture, crossing over into fashion, music and television. Take, for example, a Christina Aguilera music video on MTV or VH1 or a Britney Spears concert on HBO, dripping with sexual imagery obviously borrowed from the world of adult entertainment. You will even find porn references on the TV show "Friends."

Luke Ford, who spent seven years writing an Internet gossip column about the adult entertainment industry for his own Internet website, isn't sure what to make of it.

"It's become popular, cool, acceptable in this 18-to-25 age group. My age group, I'm 37, my age group and up, we think porn is something that's shameful. But for kids half my age, they think it's cool," says Ford, who guesses it's an act of rebellion, embracing one of society's last taboos.

Ford, who is often referred to as the [conservative commentator] Matt Drudge of porn, gave *60 Minutes* a tour of a backyard porn set in a residential neighborhood of Chatsworth that has been used by porn directors for more than 20 years.

"It is just like Hollywood," he says.

Even as It Goes Mainstream, the Industry Is Still Shady

Like the porn industry itself, it becomes less glamorous the closer you get. If you take away the accountants and CEOs, you're left with a small insular world, filled with renegades and outcasts, who like to flaunt society's rules.

"They come into this industry, because this is the single easiest way that they can earn $1,000 in a day, in two hours," says Ford. "It's not like we're losing people from going to medical school or business school or becoming lawyers."

Hang around the World Modeling talent agency on Van Nuys Boulevard in Sherman Oaks and one of the first things you notice is that there is no shortage of men or women who are eager to work in the business.

"It's just fun. I think it's awesome that you, like, can be, like, a sex icon. I think girls will argue that it's a bad thing, [but] you're crazy," says Destiny. "Because, you know, everybody thinks you're beautiful. Everybody wants to meet you."

You'll also see why Fortune 500 companies making millions off the industry don't like to be publicly associated with it.

"Most girls who enter this industry do one video and quit. The experience is so painful, horrifying, embarrassing, humiliating for them that they never do it again," says Ford.

The argument that pornography exploits women has long been one of the flashpoints for social debates about the industry. Now, antiporn groups say hundreds of thousands of men have become addicted to it, leading to antisocial behavior, and causing divorce and family breakups.

A Summary War on Smut

"Just because this material is available, and citizens tolerate it, doesn't mean that they accept it," says Mary Beth Buchanan, the U.S. attorney for the western district of Pennsylvania, and the point person in the Justice Department's campaign to rein in pornography.

When John Ashcroft was appointed attorney general, among his first acts were to hang blue drapes in front of a topless statue in the lobby of the Justice Department, and to promise a crackdown on smut.

Buchanan's prosecution of a California company called Extreme Associates is the first major obscenity case brought by the federal government in more than a decade.

"We have just had a proliferation of this type of material that has been getting increasingly worse and worse. And that's why it's important to enforce the law, and to show the producers that there are limits. There are limits to what they can sell and distribute throughout the country," says Buchanan.

She believes that three films produced and distributed by Extreme Associates by mail and over the Internet contain coercive and violent sex, along with other material that is vile and degrading.

Rob Black, president of Extreme Associates, considers that a compliment.

One film, called *Forced Entry*, includes shots of women getting raped and murdered. It also includes suffocation, strangulation, beatings and urination. Black calls *Forced Entry* a slasher film with sex, loosely based on the Hillside Strangler case. But *60 Minutes* couldn't find enough plot to show anything [on television] beyond the opening credits.

"They made absolutely no attempt to comply with federal law. In fact, it was probably their intent not to," says Buchanan. "Because what they wanted to do was to make the most disgusting material available on the market. And they succeeded."

What is federal law on pornography? The only explicit, hard-core sexual material that is absolutely illegal by law in the U.S. today is child pornography—all other material must be put before a jury.

The Supreme Court last defined obscenity as material appealing to a degrading interest in sex, depicting it in a patently offensive manner, and lacking any serious artistic, literary, or scientific value. But this was way back in 1973, before the VCR and the Internet were in existence. . . .

Buchanan says it's not the Justice Department's intention to shut down the adult entertainment industry, or eliminate all sexually explicit material—even if it could. The point is to enforce some standards, and it hopes to do so when the case against Extreme Associates finally goes to trial this fall.

Since *60 Minutes* first [aired] this report [in 2007], General Motors sold its subsidiary, Hughes [Electronics], and got out of the porn business. And actress Jenna Jameson says she wants to do the same thing: retire and become a "regular mom."

"You will be hard-pressed to find . . . towering skyscrapers wherein neatly attired businesspeople churn out . . . porn. The majority of adult video businesses are small operations run out of nondescript warehouses."

Pornography Is Not a Major Industry

Susannah Breslin

Susannah Breslin is a photographer and journalist known for her writing on sex, sexuality, and the media. She regularly blogs for Forbes.com, *and has written for* Details, Newsweek, *and* Esquire.com. *In the following viewpoint, Breslin argues that pornography has never been the $10 billion industry it has been made out to be, and that whatever market share it really had—likely never more than $1 or $2 billion—has been steadily eaten up by online piracy, armatures, and the many small players who produce a little content and then fizzle.*

As you read, consider the following questions:

1. Mainstream news stories often report that pornography is a $10–14 billion industry. What is the source of this claim? Is that a reliable source, according to Breslin?

2. How much did San Fernando Valley pornographers see their profits drop in 2009, as reported by Breslin?

3. According to the author, what measures do pornography producers take to protect the health and safety of their performers? Are these efforts sufficient?

True or false?

- The porn business generates some $10 billion to $14 billion a year in annual sales and is a "bigger business than professional football, basketball, and baseball put together."

- The porn business is a business like any other.

- That a series of adult movie production companies in Southern California's San Fernando Valley recently halted production after an unnamed adult performer tested positive for HIV is evidence that the industry is more responsible and ethical than mainstream businesses.

If you answered "true" to any of the above, you'd be dead wrong. In fact, the business of making porn is a business like no other, and if there's anything the adult movie industry has excelled at in recent years—while its profits have plummeted—it's convincing the public that it's a legitimate business. In reality, it's anything but.

Never a Major Industry, but Disseminated by the Internet

For starters, *Forbes* debunked the widely disseminated myth of the porn business raking in as much as $14 billion a year in sales back in 2001. That unsourced number was pulled from a 1998 Forrester Research study on online adult content and was mentioned in passing. So how much money do Americans spend buying and renting adult movies? The answer: Nobody knows. The megabillion-dollar numbers you see repeated in the mainstream media come from *Adult Video News*, the porn industry's trade magazine, well known for its propensity to exaggerate pretty much everything having to do with porn.

Since, the bottom has dropped out of the adult video business. The widespread availability of low-cost video cameras meant anyone who could afford one could make a porn movie, and the market was quickly saturated with adult content. Contrary to the popular belief that pornographers have remained ahead of the curve when it comes to technology, early on, pornographers failed to recognize the threat that the Internet posed to their businesses, and online content pirating hit the industry hard. A series of federal obscenity indictments under the [George W.] Bush administration also induced a chilling effect in Porn Valley that didn't help matters. By the spring of 2009, most adult directors and producers that I spoke with told me they were seeing profits dropping by 30% to 50% across the board, and adult companies were folding left and right.

While some porn companies, such as Private Media Group and New Frontier Media, operate like any other business, most aren't run like Fortune 500 companies. In truth, much of the porn business operates a lot more like the drug business. You will be hard-pressed to find pristine halls in towering skyscrapers wherein neatly attired businesspeople churn out reams of porn. The majority of adult video businesses are small operations run out of nondescript warehouses on unremarkable streets in the northwest corner of the San Fernando Valley.

A Chaotic Business

I visited one such business last year. In the foyer, there was an abandoned desk and a candy machine. In the next room,

A Tiny Industry

What pornography lacks in cultural resonance, it also lacks in financial clout. The industry is tiny next to broadcast television ($32.3 billion in 1999 revenue, according to Veronis Suhler [Stevenson]), cable television ($45.5 billion), the newspaper business ($27.5 billion), Hollywood ($31 billion), even to professional and educational publishing ($14.8 billion).

When one really examines the numbers, the porn industry—while a subject of fascination—is every bit as marginal as it seems at first glance.

Dan Ackman,
"How Big Is Porn?," Forbes.com,
May 25, 2001. www.forbes.com.

there was a green pleather sofa with a box on it that contained two lifelike silicone breasts. The handwritten sign on the door of director and producer Jim Powers' office read, "Do not ask Jim to borrow money!!! I mean it!" When I took a tour through the adjoining warehouse, DVDs spilled out of brown boxes, a giant vagina costume hung from the rafters, and little stirred amid the dust.

There are those who are in porn because they love porn, actresses who star in X-rated movies because they love the sex, and bigger adult video production companies like Vivid [Entertainment] and Wicked Pictures that are run like legitimate businesses. But by and large, they aren't the rule. In porn, businesses come and go, as do its performers. One day, I suspect the porn industry's rise and fall will look a lot like the business of selling crack in Oakland in the '80s. For a while, business was booming. Until it wasn't.

It's commendable that a handful of companies have stopped production while performers who came into direct or secondhand contact with the HIV-positive colleague are tested, but it's too little too late. Most porn companies don't require performers to use condoms on set, putting their workers at risk. Those who make porn usually believe the presence of prophylactics kills the fantasy for the viewer at home. Performers are required to get tested for HIV every 30 days and must present a valid test before they go to work in front of the cameras. But this rule isn't always enforced. A few performers have been caught faking tests. Every few years, it seems, another performer turns up HIV positive.

When it comes to the oftentimes messy business of making hard-core movies—where body fluids are exchanged like workplace e-mails—anything goes, and ethical business practices get lost in the chase for the almighty, increasingly elusive porn dollar.

> *"Sex crime investigators . . . say the breadth of what is available online, the anonymity the Internet provides and its omnipresence . . . escalate [porn] beyond a problem."*

Online Pornography Encourages Criminality

Tabatha Wethal

Tabatha Wethal is an associate editor at Law Enforcement Technology *magazine and Officer.com; she frequently writes on crime, culture, law enforcement, and the law. In the following viewpoint, she explores how the ever-present opportunity to view and collect pornography—made possible by the Internet and ever-advancing communications technologies—can reinforce deviant and criminal behavior, or even help it flourish. These same technologies have also made it next to impossible for law enforcement to monitor sex offenders and prevent them from offending again.*

Tabatha Wethal, "The Problem with Porn: The Ubiquitous, Nearly Unregulable Access to e-Porn Complicates Fighting Online Porn Addiction and Offender Monitoring," *Law Enforcement Technology*, vol. 37, no. 2, May 2011, p. 18(6). Copyright © 2011 by Cygnus Business Media. All rights reserved. Reproduced by permission.

As you read, consider the following questions:

1. Is pornography addiction listed among the disorders described in the most recent edition of the American Psychiatric Association's *Diagnostic and Statistical Manual of Mental Disorders?*

2. According to a report from comScore Media Metrix, what percentage of Internet users visited adult websites in December 2005?

3. Is it intrinsically dangerous to view pornographic images, according to Detective Nick Boffi?

In 1989, a famous self-proclaimed pornography addict described his relationship with sexually explicit materials and how he believes it related to his homicidal criminal acts in an interview:

> As a young boy of 12 or 13, I encountered, outside the home . . . soft-core pornography. Young boys explore the sideways and byways of their neighborhoods, and in our neighborhood, people would dump the garbage. From time to time, we would come across books of a harder nature— more graphic. This also included detective magazines, etc. The most damaging kind of pornography—and I'm talking from hard, real, personal experience—is that, that involves violence and sexual violence. The wedding of those two forces—as I know only too well—brings about behavior that is too terrible to describe.
>
> . . . I'm not blaming pornography. I'm not saying it caused me to go out and do certain things. I take full responsibility for all the things that I've done. That's not the question here. The issue is how this kind of literature contributed and helped mold and shape the kinds of violent behavior.

Online Porn's Powerful Influence

The now infamous interview was recorded on the eve prior to Ted Bundy's execution 21 years ago. Bundy is thought to have killed at least 28 young women and girls. He was finally convicted and sentenced to death for killing a 12-year-old girl and dumping her body in a pig sty. Though this story is an extreme example representing a convicted killer's opinion on how pornography affected his criminal compulsions, it shouldn't be discounted. Much of what Bundy relates in the interview with Dr. James Dobson, a psychologist and founder of Focus on the Family, mirrors the story of other porn addicts.

In our contemporary world of tech saturation, with folks finding their entertainment, socializing, work and play online, there exists a whole new influencing factor that wasn't around in Bundy's time: the Internet. Sex crime investigators and a recovering porn addict say the breadth of what is available online, the anonymity the Internet provides and its omnipresence . . . escalate [porn] beyond a problem.

Internet Becomes Obsession, and Then Addiction

Another man's tale begins eerily similar to a man who was killed in order to protect society. Michael Leahy explains how for him, simple pornography use became addictive.

Leahy, today in his 50s, got his foot in the door early in what would become the technological boom of the late '80s and into the '90s. Just out of college and married to his college sweetheart, Leahy says he began to indulge in online pornography that would later take from him all the foundations he had laid up until that point.

"There's no warning label on this stuff," Leahy says.

In the 1990s, Leahy was an all-American man with a storybook life: college graduate, married to his college love, starting their family and making his living at the technological giant IBM. But it wouldn't be long before Leahy fell under the spell of what he now touts as the all-American fixation: pornography online.

He considers himself a recovering pornography addict. However, according to the classifications used by mental health professionals in the United States, pornography and sex [addiction] have yet to be written into the *Diagnostic and Statistical Manual of Mental Disorders* (DSM), published by the American Psychiatric Association [APA], and their diagnostic criteria defined.

Leahy says that like some individuals casually seeking out porn through the Internet, he became obsessed with online porn in a way that would cost him his family and relationships.

The self-professed former porn addict and author of *Porn Nation: Conquering America's # 1 Addiction* and two other tomes on the subject, now makes his living speaking about his path toward addiction, recovery and the plague that he says is taking over America's computers. He tours college campuses around the world, warning of the dangers of porn.

Leahy has never committed a sex crime, but he acknowledges that his addiction had lead him to undertake unlawful behaviors, such as voyeurism and exhibitionism, when he would masturbate in the window of a motel during business trips, peering into neighboring buildings to stare at women and allowing for himself to potentially be seen.

Leahy had first experienced porn magazines as a child and had occasionally picked them up throughout his teenage and college years.

"I had a fascination with voyeurism and exhibitionism when I was very young," Leahy explains. "I had even experimented with that and had a lot of fantasy about that but never really [had] seen any material on it. Before the Internet, my diet was pretty steadily made up of *Playboy* or an occasional *Penthouse* [where] you didn't see those kinds of scenarios." But when he began working for IBM, he had a whole new influencing factor to increase what he calls his "relationship with the material." As an employee, Leahy had access to a higher-speed connection at work than most Internet-capable homes during that time, enabling him a doorway to what was quickly becoming a vast stockpile of images online without the risk of getting caught with explicit material.

"When I got on the Internet and started finding these voyeurism sites and exhibitionism sites and all these other categories of things that I never even knew existed, it really increased the amount of sexual stimulation that I started to experience," Leahy says. "A person usually has a certain [penchant] for something. For some, it's children—child pornography. . . . For others it may be exposing themselves or exhibitionism or voyeurism, that whole deal. So that's where this really crosses over from being something where you're abusing yourself to something that's abusing others."

Patterns of Deviance Leading to Crimes

Nick Boffi, a Fairfax County, Va., detective working in the child exploitation units for about five years for a total of 17 combined years with the department, says he has seen similar step-by-step transitions take place with the child enticement cases he has worked over the last few years.

"Many of my cases start out with just child pornography," Boffi says. "That didn't do it for [the offenders] anymore and they moved on to the actual enticement.

"The reason they're going for the enticement is that they're not getting the thrill of looking at the child porn, they actually want to participate in some sort of act."

He explains that though he would not lump all cases and all offenders into this category, he's seen a pattern form over years.

"That's just statistics; that's not saying that yes, 100 percent of the time [a suspect enticing a child online will] have child pornography," Boffi says. "But in order to quench their thirst before actually doing the enticement, they're building up their fantasy by looking at the child pornography. And then they go the next step with the child enticement."

Leahy says he became dissatisfied with his sex life and began consuming porn regularly at work until eventually, like Bundy mentions, the fantasy was not enough to quench his sexual thirst and Leahy began having extramarital affairs to satisfy his sexual appetite. Leahy's addiction did not drive him to break any laws—his affairs were with consenting adults. But Leahy acknowledges that Bundy's 1989 pornography confessions sound a little too familiar for comfort.

"You reach a point where the pornography only goes so far, you reach that jumping-off point where you begin to wonder if maybe actually doing it would give that which is beyond just reading it or looking at it," Bundy says in the 1989 interview. Like for Bundy, the material acted as a stepping stone into a realm where Leahy says he broke his moral codes, acts like masturbating in a window and having an extramarital affair that he had not thought he was capable of before he built an appetite for it through viewing online erotica.

Convenience and Anonymity Lead to Dependence

The Internet is not the problem, it is excessive user behavior that starts the ball rolling toward addiction. It's difficult to pin down an exact figure of how vast the online porn world is. According to one news source, every second more than 28,000 Internet users are viewing it and 372 people are using search engines to find it (2009 CNBC.com report). According to a survey, there are almost 40 million users; other estimates pin porn as about 40 percent of all Internet traffic; and various sources between 2001 to 2007 estimate revenue anywhere from $1 to $14 billion, depending on the source. According to comScore Media Metrix, there were 63.4 million unique visitors to adult websites in December of 2005, reaching 37 per-

Online Pornography Perverts Child Development

In addition to the physical and emotional injuries suffered by children who are lured into the production of child pornography is the psychological harm to children who are exposed to pornographic images of both adults and children on the Internet. Some minors seek out this material, which is readily available online, without realizing the harm they may be inflicting upon themselves. Other children are involuntarily exposed to harmful images. . . . Early introduction to such graphic images can damage the normal course of a child's sexual orientation. This is a depraved method of inducting children into abnormal sexual behaviors and conditioning them to violent and degrading images.

Margaret C. Jasper,
The Law of Obscenity and Pornography.
New York: Oceana, 2009.

cent of the Internet audience. A Family Safe Media figure puts 2006 Internet porn revenue at 32.84 million. What can be derived from these figures is that if they're within the ballpark of the true numbers, online porn is big business and growing.

Boffi says that the most common form of pornography he encounters is digital. In investigating cases through the child enticement unit, Boffi says he rarely sees a stash of snapshots, but rather the collector has built an electronic image base.

"It's very rare, unless the person is an older person, that they have actual photographs," Boffi says. "With the access to the Internet, it's just as easy to collect the child pornography online. It's an easier way to manage it, maintain it and also give some kind of privacy, as opposed to having just pictures lying around the house."

Leahy says he was able to feed his appetite for viewing (legal) pornography because of the anonymity and nearly risk-free forum of electronic porn. Even in the early days, Leahy explained, individuals would have to transport porn onto CD-ROMs and floppy disks. Today's capabilities include wireless technology access and handheld devices, creating one's own portable peep show, and producing what Leahy dubs a perfect storm for excessive, addictive behaviors to develop.

Online Porn and Advancing Technology Make It Impossible to Monitor Sex Offenders

Today's Internet ecosystem has another influencing factor that did not exist when Leahy was at his heaviest level of porn consumption—mobile Internet access and portable storage devices. These new ways to view and collect Internet smut via smartphones like an iPhone or BlackBerry can help criminals evade discovery from spouses and family, and for monitored convicted offenders to elude supervising authorities from detecting it. Wireless access to the Internet makes it easy to access and download portable e-Porn on devices to take anywhere.

The portable Internet access and myriad ways to connect are what complicate the monitoring of convicted offenders. Attempts to collect passwords, control environment (no computer/Internet in home) are nearly worthless, as the ubiquity of computing and Internet access make home supervision moot.

Boffi says Fairfax County monitors approximately 600 sex offenders. Boffi's unit primarily performs work and home verification checks on the county's registered offenders to be sure they are reporting to the county truthfully. Though he is not a probation agent, when he has accompanied officers on home visits, he says he doesn't recall finding any contraband.

He says that if the offender wanted to view porn or start a child porn archive, the ways to evade discovery are too easy.

Leahy says for a recovering sex or pornography addict, slipping back into old habits is always a concern. Without making that restricted individual accountable for his or her online activity, the temptation could be too great. And all sources agree that evading detection of prohibited use is far too easy in this digital climate.

If the individual really wanted to, he or she could go to a library or to a friend's house to use the Internet. They could also hide a laptop or smartphone when the probation officer's coming over. Boffi adds that though the probation officer can search through anything, the ability [of offenders] to hide small, portable devices works against them.

"Think about how small electronic devices are, like a thumb drive," Boffi says. "If you had a thumb drive that you downloaded child pornography on and just slipped it in a junk drawer of a kitchen. Thumb drives are small enough that we're going to miss that. Unless we're specifically looking for that thumb drive and know kind of where it's at, we're going to miss that in a cursory search."

Online Porn Can Contribute to Criminal Obsessions

The debate over whether online pornography is the cause of serious societal ills, or merely harmless entertainment, is not without its opposition. Some groups say online porn is not a problem and actively engage in public discussions to argue their respective sides. Ron Jeremy, porn actor and industry figurehead who has engaged in multiple public debates, including some with Leahy, campaigns for the pro-porn argument. Jeremy says porn is not the problem. From 2007 to 2009, he was part of a pornography debate tour dubbed the "XXX Porn Debate" that tackled the porn issue. Representatives from companies that deliver adult content on the Internet have long argued that their programming contributes to healthy relationships and can be educational.

Nick Boffi says that pornography isn't innately a problem. In fact, he says regular, noncriminal consumption of online pornography can be a normal part of life.

"Just viewing regular pornography, even in excess, is not going to make someone do something they don't want to do," he explains. But he emphasizes that there is no casual use of sexual images of children. "Just possessing it, [that person is] already committing a crime and getting a thrill out of that," he explains. "And once that thrill runs out they're going to look for an additional thrill, which would be the meeting of a kid or the actual committing of an abuse, like taking their own photographs and posting them."

Leahy has remarried and rebuilt the relationships he lost due to his addiction. He has been on a mission to maintain sobriety from porn and raise awareness of the issue since 2000. He works mentoring others who say they've become addicted to pornography or sex as well. He reveals that realizing how his noncriminal addictive behaviors echoed those of convicts like Ted Bundy remind him of the danger he believes online porn poses.

Though every pornography consumer's story does not reach the level of homicidal criminal acts that Bundy's did, sex crime task force specialists and a recovering addict allow that online pornography may influence criminal sexual activity in a harmful way. Leahy is still hoping the APA will recognize sex and porn addiction in the DSM, the standard classification of mental disorders and their diagnostic criteria used by mental health professionals, and says he'll consider that a win for the fight against online deviant sexual behavior and related criminal activity.

"As raunch has waxed, rape has waned."

Access to Online Pornography Reduces Rape

Steve Chapman

Steve Chapman is a columnist and editorial writer for the Chicago Tribune. In the following viewpoint, Chapman argues that as pornography has increased with the advent of the Internet, violent sexual assault has decreased. While in the past some feminists have argued that pornography can cause sexual assault, Chapman points to recent research by Todd Kendall, an economics professor at Clemson University, that suggests the opposite may be true. In his research, Kendall found that increased Internet access within a state tended to correlate with a declining incidence of rape, even as other violent crimes remained steady. Chapman explains Kendall's research indicates pornography may serve as a "substitute" for committing an actual act of sexual violence.

As you read, consider the following questions:

1. According to the author, violent crime has dropped by how much since 1993?

2. Why, according to the author, can the decline in sexual assault not be contributed to underreporting?

3. Todd Kendall's research proves what plays a big role in the incidence of rape, according to the author?

In the 1980s, conservatives and feminists joined to fight a common nemesis: the spread of pornography. Unlike past campaigns to stamp out smut, this one was based not only on morality but also on public safety. They argued that hard-core erotica was intolerable because it promoted sexual violence against women.

Linking Pornography and Sexual Assault

"Pornography is the theory; rape is the practice," wrote feminist author Robin Morgan. In 1986, a federal commission concurred. Some kinds of pornography, it concluded, are bound to lead to "increased sexual violence." Indianapolis passed a law allowing women to sue producers for sexual assaults caused by material depicting women in "positions of servility or submission or display."

The campaign fizzled when the courts said the ordinance was an unconstitutional form of "thought control." Though the [George W.] Bush administration has put new emphasis on prosecuting obscenity, on the grounds that it fosters violence against women, pornography is more available now than ever.

That's due in substantial part to the rise of the Internet, where the United States alone has a staggering 244 million Web pages featuring erotic fare. One Nielsen survey found that one out of every four users say they visited adult sites in the last month.

So in the last two decades, we have conducted a vast experiment on the social consequences of such material. If the supporters of censorship were right, we should be seeing an

Using Pornography Is a Poor Predictor of Future Criminal Behavior

[Researchers] found that rapists were more likely than non-rapists in the prison population to have been punished for looking at pornography while a youngster, ... [and] that incarcerated non-rapists had seen more pornography, and seen it at an earlier age, than rapists. What does correlate highly with sex offense is a strict, repressive religious upbringing. [Other studies found] that both rapists and child molesters use less pornography than a control group of "normal" males.

Milton Diamond, "Porn: Good for Us?,"
The Scientist, March 1, 2010.

unparalleled epidemic of sexual assault. But all the evidence indicates they were wrong. As raunch has waxed, rape has waned.

A Decline in Sexual Assault

This is part of a broad decrease in criminal mayhem. Since 1993, violent crime in America has dropped by 58 percent. But the progress in this one realm has been especially dramatic. Rape is down 72 percent and other sexual assaults have fallen by 68 percent. Even in the last two years, when the FBI reported upticks in violent crime, the number of rapes continued to fall.

Nor can the decline be dismissed as the result of underreporting. Many sexual assaults do go unreported, but there is no reason to think there is less reporting today than in the past. In fact, given everything that has been done to educate people about the problem and to prosecute offenders, victims are probably more willing to come forward [now] than they used to be.

No one would say the current level of violence against women is acceptable. But the enormous progress in recent years is one of the most gratifying successes imaginable.

How can it be explained? Perhaps the most surprising and controversial account comes from Clemson University economist Todd Kendall, who suggests that adult fare on the Internet may essentially inoculate against sexual assaults.

Pornography May Help Decrease Sexual Assault

In a paper presented at Stanford Law School last year [2006], he reported that, after adjusting for other differences, states where Internet access expanded the fastest saw rape decline the most. A 10 percent increase in Internet access, Kendall found, typically meant a 7.3 percent reduction in the number of reported rapes. For other types of crime, he found no correlation with Web use. What this research suggests is that sexual urges play a big role in the incidence of rape—and that pornographic Web sites provide a harmless way for potential predators to satisfy those desires.

That, of course, is only a theory, and the evidence he cites is not conclusive. States that were quicker to adopt the Internet may be different in ways that also serve to prevent rape. It's not hard to think of other explanations why sexual assaults have diminished so rapidly—such as DNA analysis, which has been an invaluable tool in catching and convicting offenders.

Changing social attitudes doubtless have also played a role. Both young men and young women are more aware today of the boundaries between consensual and coercive sex. Kim Gandy, president of the National Organization for Women, thinks the credit for progress against rape should go to federal funding under the Violence Against Women Act and to education efforts stressing that "no means no."

But if expanding the availability of hard-core fare doesn't prevent rapes, we can be confident from the experience of recent years that it certainly doesn't cause such crimes. Whether you think porn is a constitutionally protected form of expression or a vile blight that should be eradicated, this discovery should come as very good news.

"Picture an addiction so lethal it has the potential to render an entire generation incapable of forming lasting marriages."

Online Pornography Negatively Changes How People Form Relationships

National Review Online

The anonymous author of this viewpoint, which appeared in the National Review Online, is a psychologist who lives with her five children in Virginia. In the following viewpoint, she recounts how her husband's obsession with online pornography shattered his life and destroyed their marriage of thirteen years. The author argues that the prevalence and extreme stimulation inherent in online pornography has significantly disrupted many American marriages and is wreaking long-term havoc on Americans' capacity to form meaningful, stable relationships. She ultimately concludes that the mainstream assumption that pornography should be considered protected speech under the First Amendment creates serious obstacles to addressing this growing crisis.

As you read, consider the following questions:

1. What are the four stages of pornography addiction identified by Dr. Victor Cline?

2. What is the likelihood that an Internet user who has cheated on his or her spouse has also indulged in online pornography, compared to Internet users who have never had an extramarital affair?

3. According to the American Academy of Matrimonial Lawyers, in what percentage of divorce cases does "an obsessive interest in Internet pornography" play a significant role?

Imagine a drug so powerful it can destroy a family simply by distorting a man's perception of his wife. Picture an addiction so lethal it has the potential to render an entire generation incapable of forming lasting marriages and so widespread that it produces more annual revenue—$97 billion worldwide in 2006—than all of the leading technology companies combined. Consider a narcotic so insidious that it evades serious scientific study and legislative action for decades, thriving instead under the ever-expanding banner of the First Amendment.

A Story of Addiction

According to an online statistics firm, an estimated 40 million people use this drug on a regular basis. It doesn't come in pill form. It can't be smoked, injected, or snorted. And yet neurological data suggest its effects on the brain are strikingly similar to those of synthetic drugs. Indeed, two authorities on the neurochemistry of addiction, Harvey Milkman and Stanley Sunderwirth, claim it is the ability of this drug to influence all three pleasure systems in the brain—arousal, satiation, and fantasy—that makes it "the *pièce de résistance* among the addictions."

Earlier this month [March 2010], the Witherspoon Institute released a report examining "The Social Costs of Pornography," signed by more than 50 scholars representing a wide array of professions, academic disciplines, and political views. The report details the considerable social costs that pornography exacts upon men, women, and children.

The findings of the report hit particularly close to home for me. By his own account, my husband of 13 years and high-school sweetheart was first exposed to pornography around age ten. He viewed it regularly during high school and college—and, although he tried hard to stop, continued to do so throughout the course of our marriage. For the past few years he had taken to sleeping in the basement, distancing himself from me, emotionally and physically. Recently he began to reject my sexual advances outright, claiming he just didn't "feel love" for me like he used to, and lamenting that he thought of me "more as the mother of our children" than as a sexual partner.

Then one morning around 2AM he called, intoxicated, from his office to announce that he had "developed feelings" for someone new. The woman he became involved with was an unemployed alcoholic with all the physical qualities of a porn star—bleached blond hair, heavy makeup, provocative clothing, and large breasts. After the revelation, my husband tried to break off his relationship with this woman. But his remorse was short-lived. Within a few months he had moved permanently out of the home he shared with me and our five young children. In retrospect, I believe he succumbed to the allure of the secret fantasy life he had been indulging since his adolescence.

The Four Phases of Porn Addiction

My husband is not alone. According to Dr. Victor Cline, a nationally renowned clinical psychologist who specializes in sexual addiction, pornography addiction is a process that un-

Internet Porn Can Replace Real Relationships

Though porn research is the subject of much debate and barb-flinging ..., scientists speculate that a dopamine-oxytocin combo is released in the brain during orgasm, acting as a "biochemical love potion," as behavioral therapist Andrea Kuszewski calls it. It's the reason after having sex with someone, you're probably more inclined to form an emotional attachment. But you don't have to actually have sex in order to get those neurotransmitters firing. When you watch porn, "you're bonding with it," Kuszewski says. "And those chemicals make you want to keep coming back to have that feeling." Which allows men ... to potentially develop a neurological attachment to it. They can, in essence, date porn.

Davy Rothbart,
"He's Just Not That into Anyone,"
New York, *January 30, 2011.*

dergoes four phases. First, addiction, resulting from early and repeated exposure accompanied by masturbation. Second, escalation, during which the addict requires more frequent porn exposure to achieve the same "highs" and may learn to prefer porn to sexual intercourse. Third, desensitization, during which the addict views as normal what was once considered repulsive or immoral. And finally, the acting-out phase, during which the addict runs an increased risk of making the leap from screen to real life.

This behavior may manifest itself in the form of promiscuity, voyeurism, exhibitionism, group sex, rape, sadomasochism, or even child molestation. The final phase may also be characterized by one or more extramarital affairs. A 2004 study published in *Social Science Quarterly* found that Internet users who had had an extramarital affair were 3.18 times more likely to have used online porn than Internet users who had not had an affair. Among other things, the Witherspoon report is a stern warning to all married women to take seriously the signs of a sexual addiction, before it is too late.

Pornography Erodes Relationships

Perhaps the greatest hardship for women who fear they have lost (or are losing) a husband to Internet porn is the absence of a public consensus about the harmful effects of pornography *on marriage*. Consider what we know. In a study published in *Sexual Addiction and Compulsivity*, [Jennifer P.] Schneider found that among the 68 percent of couples in which one person was addicted to Internet porn, one or both had lost interest in sex. Results of the same study, published in 2000, indicated that porn use was a major contributing factor to increased risk of separation and divorce. This finding is substantiated by results of a 2002 meeting of the American Academy of Matrimonial Lawyers, during which surveyed lawyers claimed that "an obsessive interest in Internet pornography" was a significant factor in 56 percent of their divorce cases the prior year.

Porn use creates the impression that aberrant sexual practices are more common than they really are, and that promiscuous behavior is normal. For example, in a 2000 meta-analysis of 46 published studies put out by the National Foundation for Family Research and Education at the University of Calgary, regular exposure to pornography increased risk of sexual deviancy (including lower age of first intercourse and excessive masturbation), increased belief in the "rape myth" (that women cause rape and rapists are normal), and was associated with negative attitudes regarding intimate relationships (e.g., rejecting the need for courtship and viewing persons as sexual objects). Indeed, neurological imaging confirms the latter finding. Susan Fiske, professor of psychology at Princeton University, used MRI [magnetic resonance imaging] scans to analyze the brain activity of men viewing pornography. She found that after viewing porn, men looked at women more as objects than as human beings.

Cultural Hurdles Prevent Treating Porn Addiction

The social implications of these data are significant, but we need to know more. The American Psychiatric Association is likely to add pornography addiction to their *Diagnostic and Statistical Manual [of Mental Disorders]* this year. Congress should fund a long-term, multidisciplinary analysis of the effects of porn addiction on marriage and family life. The National Institutes of Health are granted billions of taxpayer dollars for research on a wide variety of public health problems, and yet pornography addiction is not among them. Most health insurance companies provide little to no coverage for treatment of this problem, and the health care legislation signed into law last week promises more of the same. The fact is that the moral and financial needs of couples struggling with this form of addiction will remain unaddressed in a country that views pornography use as a constitutional right.

I will never know with full certainty that pornography caused my husband to abandon me and our children. Although I loved him deeply, I was far from a perfect wife. In retrospect, I wish I had understood what he was experiencing and had acted to help him. If anything is clear to me, it is this: We must learn more about this scourge and its effects on families. The Witherspoon report makes it clear that countless women—and increasingly many men—have experienced the devastating effects of their spouse's pornography use. Countless more will experience it in the future. It is our obligation as a nation to pursue the truth for their sake, no matter how inconvenient for some the verdict may be.

> *"The opportunity the Web has provided for people to make and access more diverse representations and views of sex can only be viewed as a positive thing."*

Online Pornography Has Positively Affected Views of Sex and Sexuality

Aleks Krotoski

Aleks Krotoski is known for her writing on technology, culture, and interactivity. The following viewpoint is drawn from her blog Untangling the Web, *which documents the interviews and other background research she uses for her technology and culture column for the* Observer, *a British newspaper. In this interview, the author talks with Feona Attwood, editor of* Porn.com: Making Sense of Online Pornography *and* Mainstreaming Sex: The Sexualization of Western Culture. *In the following viewpoint, Attwood points out that the Internet has not fundamentally changed pornography, but rather it has broadened access both for consumers and producers, especially opening up pornography for and by women.*

Aleks Krotoski, "Interview: Professor Feona Attwood, Author, Porn.com," untanglingthe web.tumblr.com, February 2, 2011. Copyright © 2011 by Aleks Krotoski. All rights reserved. Reproduced by permission.

As you read, consider the following questions:

1. According to the Australian research recounted in *The Porn Report*, how did people who used porn believe it affected their lives?

2. According to Feona Attwood, how has online pornography changed the public conversation about sex and sexuality? Is this change positive or negative?

3. Does Attwood suspect that online porn's influence on mainstream discussions of sex will be a short-lived fad, or will it have a lasting impact? How?

Most of the dialogue in the mainstream media about online sexuality tends to focus on access to porn and kinks, and particularly their problematic aspects. But what evidence is there that Web porn and kink exposure has actually affected our sexual attitudes and behaviours?

I spoke with Professor Feona Attwood, Principal Lecturer in Communication at Sheffield Hallam University and editor of *Porn.com: [Making Sense of Online Pornography]*, a collection of research from academic specialists in this field published in 2009. Here, she discusses the ways in which the Web is making a difference in terms of production and consumption of explicit sexual material, its long-term effects on the sexual evolution of today's media-savvy young adults, and—importantly—how online porn is no different from porn in other media.

Aleks Krotoski: What are the practices, styles and cultures of online porn? How are these distinctive from porn in other media?

Feona Attwood: What's now available online is making us think again about what porn is. For example, you'll find many of the same things online as you will in other media—classic films, genres like gonzo, pinup pictures—but what's also out there are amateur scenes in domestic settings; queer, kinky and feminist pornographies; subcultural and indie productions; lots of erotic and pornographic storytelling; practices which mix the sexual display we associate with porn with dating or social networking (for example on swinging or 'rate-me' sites). It's this variety really that's so distinctive about porn in an online setting.

How has the Web changed the production and consumption of porn?

It's made both much easier in terms of entry level to production and ease and anonymity of consumption.

It's no longer really possible to talk about a porn 'industry' as though this was an identifiable and monolithic thing; alongside the big companies like Vivid [Entertainment] there are now loads of smaller producers and there's tons of amateur material online.

In terms of consumption, the most striking thing for me is the way porn has become accessible to women; earlier forms of porn distribution which relied on visits to sex shops or on porn being passed among men made it really difficult for women to get hold of porn, as well as all kinds of other sex products. The Web has made it possible for women to access porn easily, which is hugely important for the way porn will develop in the future.

What effect has an increase in access to pornography via the Web had on our off-line attitudes to sex, and to our sexual behaviours? How has it altered what sex means?

There's extraordinarily little research on the way we interact with porn. There's only one major study that's been carried out with actual audiences of porn—in Australia a few years ago and written up in a book called *The Porn Report* (2008)—and this found that people who used porn thought it was largely beneficial in their sex lives; but this study didn't really focus on online porn. So we haven't had much evidence to help us think this question through.

This year [2011] though, a major new research project on porn audiences, led by Dr. Clarissa Smith and using online questionnaires, is being launched, and I think this will make a huge contribution to our knowledge. What we also know is that using online porn is part of a broader move towards bringing technology into our sex lives and one that you can already see in the way sex is discussed. For example, many sex advice guides often assume we might want to use toys and porn, take photographs and make films as part of our sexual repertoire. And the way that people now interact sexually online suggests a mixing of sex with media and technology. Both these developments suggest a big shift around what sex is, how you can do it and what it means.

How much has Web access to porn assisted in the 'mainstreaming' of sex and sexual kinks, in comparison with other media?

British culture has been fascinated by talking about sex for a very long time and in that sense sex has been a pretty visible subject for mainstream consideration. Older media have often been dominated by a view of sex as scandalous and dangerous, but on the whole their own depictions of sex have been pretty predictable. Access to a more diverse set of representations—particularly pornographies, and especially kinky kinds—hasn't been possible for most people. Web access has made it possible to see a much broader variety of sexual representations than ever before. This doesn't necessarily mean that many more people are using kinky porn—though this might be the case—but it definitely does mean that different views of sexual pleasure and identity are much more visible and accessible than in the past.

What are the problematic aspects of online porn? What are the positive aspects?

The opportunity the Web has provided for people to make and access more diverse representations and views of sex can only be viewed as a positive thing. This doesn't necessarily mean that we are going to like or agree about everything that we find out there, but a grown-up society can find ways of dealing with this. The problematic aspects of any porn—online or off-line—remain what they've always been: are the people who work in porn treated fairly?, are they paid properly?, are their working conditions safe?—but these are questions that need to be asked about any form of production and indeed any kind of work.

How important is porn now to the development of sexuality and sexual practices in the media-savvy young generations, versus the pre-Web generations?

There are more young adults out there making porn for their own generation, and given that media and technology are such an important part of the lives of young people, I think online porn is definitely going to be part of the mix in the future. What we need now is to move on from the kinds of panicked responses to online porn that we often see in the media and start to really think more broadly about how sex and sexuality—in all their aspects—are practiced, and what they mean in the twenty-first century.

Periodical and Internet Sources Bibliography

The following articles have been selected to supplement the diverse views presented in this chapter.

Marina Adshade	"Free Porn Lowers Rape Rates," Big Think, April 9, 2011. http://bigthink.com.
Jonathan Bick	"Protection of Underage Internet Users Impacts e-Commerce," *New Jersey Law Journal*, January 18, 2010.
Richard Corliss	"That Old Feeling: Porn Again," *Time*, May 7, 2005.
Milton Diamond	"Porn: Good for Us?," *The Scientist*, March 1, 2010.
Gail Dines	"Yes, Pornography Is Racist," *Ms. Magazine Blog*, August 27, 2010. http://msmagazine.com/blog.
Judy Greenwald	"Workers' Misuse of Web May Create Liabilities," *Business Insurance*, October 11, 2009.
Marty Klein	"The Myth of 'Racist Pornography,'" *Psychology Today*, February 10, 2011.
Davy Rothbart	"He's Just Not That into Anyone," *New York*, January 30, 2011.
Peter Suderman	"Does More Porn Make Society Better?," *Reason*, July 15, 2009.
Gary Wilson	"WEIRD Masturbation Habits: Who Are the Solo-Sex World Champs?," Your Brain on Porn, May 14, 2011. htfp://yourbrainonporn.com.

OPPOSING
VIEWPOINTS®
SERIES

CHAPTER 2

What Is the Impact of Online Pornography on Individuals?

Chapter Preface

In the debate surrounding the impact of pornography on individuals, one question stands out, both for its frequency and its sinister implications: "Is pornography addictive?" How that question is answered deeply influences the collective understanding of pornography and how it should be treated under the law. If pornography is thought of as just pictures, sounds, and words—no different, apart from subject matter, than an action film or the catalog from a photography exhibit—then adherents to that belief would no doubt think that it should be lightly regulated at best, perhaps only so far as to guarantee that no one who works in its production is cheated or injured. If, on the other hand, pornography is more than just stimulating, but seriously habit forming—like cocaine or Adderall—then few Americans would want it accessible to anyone with a little curiosity and a computer.

At one time, the notion that pictures might function at all like cocaine would have been absurd. But recent neurological studies have more thoroughly established the function of certain hormones and neurotransmitters (especially dopamine) in the brain's "reward circuitry"—which is the underlying mechanism in chemical addictions (like cocaine addiction), long-established addiction-like behaviors such as compulsive gambling, and behaviors associated with the consumption of Internet porn. It has been established that dopamine-based responses are highly susceptible to desensitization: Gamblers "chase" ever-larger wagers, and cocaine addicts seek out either greater quantities or higher quality. Addiction "rewires" the brain's reward circuitry into a self-reinforcing—and self-destructive—loop. Drawing on this research, many pundits, cultural commentators, therapists, and activists have suggested that viewing pornography might similarly alter the brain.

While these inductive leaps have grabbed headlines and placed books on best-seller lists, they have frustrated a great many neurologists, psychologists, and psychiatric clinicians. As Vaughan Bell—a clinical and research psychologist, college professor, and research fellow with King's College London—writes, these pundits are "accidentally right when [they] say that porn 'rewires the brain' but, as everything rewires the brain, this tells us nothing. . . . Porn is portrayed as a dangerous addictive drug that hooks naive users and leads them into sexual depravity and dysfunction. The trouble is, if this is true . . . it would also be true for sex itself which relies on, unsurprisingly, a remarkably similar dopamine reward system."

In the following chapter, authors from across the cultural spectrum seek to establish not only whether or not online pornography is addictive, but also what actual risks and benefits online pornography poses to individuals.

> *"Pornography is a* visual pheromone, *a powerful . . . brain drug that is changing human sexuality by 'inhibiting orientation' and 'disrupting pre-mating communication between the sexes' . . . especially through the Internet."*

Internet Pornography Is Addictive

Donald L. Hilton Jr.

Donald L. Hilton Jr. is a neurological surgeon and the author of He Restoreth My Soul: Understanding and Breaking the Chemical and Spiritual Chains of Pornography Through the Atonement of Jesus Christ. *In the following viewpoint, Hilton argues that Internet pornography is just as addictive as artificial drugs like cocaine or methamphetamine and points out that masturbating to pornography stimulates the same pleasure circuitry in the brain as these drugs. Hilton maintains that this process causes physical changes in the brain that result in impulsivity, compulsivity, depression, and a general degradation to interpersonal relationships and quality of life.*

As you read, consider the following questions:

1. What are the four behaviors associated with frontal lobe brain damage, according to the viewpoint?

2. According to Hilton, what changes in the frontal lobes of the brain are indicative of both "chemical addictions" and "natural addiction"?

3. What are the three aspects of the "triple hook" of porn addiction, according to Hilton?

While some have avoided using the term "addiction" in the context of natural compulsions such as uncontrolled sexuality, overeating, or gambling, let us consider current scientific evidence regarding the brain and addiction.

This [viewpoint] will seek to answer two questions: (1) Biologically, is the brain affected by pornography and other sexual addictions? (2) If so, and if such addictions are widespread, can they have a societal effect as well?

Gypsy Moth (and Human) Sexuality

Let's begin with a seeming digression. In 1869 the gypsy moth was brought to America to attempt to jump-start a silk industry. Rarely have good intentions gone so wrong, as the unforeseen appetite of the moth for deciduous trees such as oaks, maples, and elms has devastated forests for 150 years. Numerous attempts were made to destroy this pest, but a major breakthrough came in the 1960s, when scientists noted that the male gypsy moth finds a female to mate with by following her scent. This scent is called a pheromone, and is extremely attractive to the male.

In 1971 a paper was published in the journal *Nature* that described how pheromones were used to prevent the moths from mating. The scientists mass-produced the pheromone and permeated the moths' environment with it. This unnaturally strong scent overpowered the females' normal ability to attract the male, and the confused males were unable to find females. A follow-up paper described how population control of the moths was achieved by "preventing male gypsy moths from finding mates."

The gypsy moth was the first insect to be controlled by the use of pheromones, which work by two methods. One is called the confusion method. An airplane scatters an environmentally insignificant number of very small plastic pellets imbedded with the scent of the pheromone. Then, as science journalist Anna Salleh describes it, "The male either becomes confused and doesn't know which direction to turn for the female, or he becomes desensitized to the lower levels of pheromones naturally given out by the female and has no incentive to mate with her."

The other method is called the trapping method: Pheromone-infused traps are set, from which moths cannot escape; a male moth enters looking for a female, only to find a fatal substitute.

What does this have to do with pornography? Pornography is a *visual pheromone*, a powerful $100 billion per year brain drug that is changing human sexuality by "inhibiting orientation" and "disrupting pre-mating communication between the sexes by permeating the atmosphere," especially through the Internet. I believe we are currently struggling in the war against pornography because many continue to believe two key fallacies:

Fallacy No. 1: Pornography is not a drug.

Fallacy No. 2: Pornography is therefore not a real addiction. . . .

Chemical Influences on the Brain

First, I would like to share an experience our family had a few years ago on a safari in Africa. While on a game drive along the Zambezi River, our ranger commented on the adrenaline grass growing along the banks. I asked him why he used the word "adrenaline," and he began to drive slowly through the grass. Abruptly, he stopped the vehicle and said, "There! Do you see it?"

"See what?" I asked. He drove closer, and this also changed the angle of the light.

Then I understood. A lion was hiding in the grass watching the river, just waiting for some "fast food" to come and get a drink.

We were sitting in an open-air Land Rover with no doors and no windows. I then understood why it was called *adrenaline grass*, as I felt my heart pound. My cerebral cortex saw and defined the danger, which registered in the autonomic, or automatic, part of my nervous system. The brain, which is a very efficient pharmaceutical lab, produced the chemical adrenaline, causing my heart to pound and race in preparation for survival. I was ready to run if needed (not that it would have done any good with the lion).

We were told that if we stayed in our seats and remained still, the lion would look at the Land Rover as a whole and not see us as individuals. Fortunately this was the case for us.

"Natural" vs. "Synthetic" Drugs

Interestingly, adrenaline, also called epinephrine, is a *drug* we physicians use in surgery and in emergencies to start a patient's heart again when it beats too slow, or even stops. So here is the question: Is epinephrine *not* a drug if the brain makes it (causing the heart to pound and race), yet *is* a drug if the same epinephrine is given by a physician?

Or consider dopamine. This chemical is a close cousin to epinephrine, both of which are excitatory neurotransmitters that tell the brain to *Go!* Dopamine is important in the parts of our brain that allow us to move, and when the dopamine-producing parts of the brain are damaged, Parkinson's disease results. To treat Parkinson's, physicians prescribe dopamine as a drug, and it helps the patient move again. So is dopamine a drug only if the pharmaceutical lab makes it, and not if the brain makes the same chemical for the same purpose?

Of course, both are drugs in every sense of the word, regardless of where they are produced. Pertinent to our subject, it happens that both of these brain drugs are very important in human sexuality—and in pornography and sexual addiction. Dopamine, in addition to its role in movement, is an integral neurotransmitter, or brain drug, in the pleasure/reward system in the brain.

Dopamine and Brain Anatomy

Let's review some of the important components of the reward system of the brain. On the outside is the cerebral cortex, a layer of nerve cells that carry conscious, volitional thought. In the front, over the eyes, are the *frontal lobes*. These areas are important in judgment, and, if the brain were a car, the frontal lobes would be the brakes. These lobes have important connections to the pleasure pathways, so pleasure can be controlled.

In the center of the brain is the *nucleus accumbens*. This almond-sized area is a key pleasure reward center, and when activated by dopamine and other neurotransmitters, it causes us to value and desire pleasure rewards. Dopamine is essential for humans to desire and value appropriate pleasure in life. Without it, we would not be as incentivized to eat, procreate, or even to try to win a game.

It's the *overuse* of the dopamine reward system that causes addiction. When the pathways are used compulsively, a downgrading occurs that actually decreases the amount of dopamine in the pleasure areas available for use, and the dopamine cells themselves start to atrophy, or shrink. The reward cells in the nucleus accumbens are now starved for dopamine and exist in a state of dopamine craving, as a downgrading of dopamine receptors on the pleasure cells occurs as well. This resetting of the "pleasure thermostat" produces a "new nor-

One Man's Account of Porn Addiction

I've been looking at Internet pornography since I began college 13 years ago. Around age 24, I noticed difficulty getting aroused with real women. Generic Viagra off the Internet allowed me to have real relationships with few problems until the age of 29. Then, it became increasingly difficult to have real sex, even with the pills.

Realizing my problem, I tried several times to give up porn. The longest I lasted without it was 3 weeks. . . . I need to be cured of this.

Marnia Robinson and Gary Wilson,
"As Porn Goes Up, Performance Goes Down?,"
Psychology Today, March 3, 2010.

mal." In this addictive state, the person must act out in addiction to boost the dopamine to levels sufficient just to feel normal.

As the desensitization of the reward circuits continues, stronger and stronger stimuli are required to boost the dopamine. In the case of narcotic addiction, the addicted person must increase the amount of the drug to get the same high. In pornography addiction, progressively more shocking images are required to stimulate the person.

Addiction Is a Form of Brain Damage

As a feedback of sorts, the frontal lobes also atrophy, or shrink. Think of it as a "wearing out of the brake pads." This physical and functional decline in the judgment center of the brain causes the person to become impaired in his ability to process the consequences of acting out in addiction. Addiction scientists have called this condition *hypofrontality*, and have noted a similarity in the behavior of addicted persons to the behavior of patients with frontal brain damage.

Neurosurgeons frequently treat people with frontal lobe damage. In a car crash, for instance, the driver's brain will often decelerate into the back of his forehead inside his skull, bruising the frontal lobes. Patients with frontal lobe damage exhibit a constellation of behaviors we call frontal lobe syndrome. First, these patients are *impulsive*, in that they thoughtlessly engage in activities with little regard to the consequences. Second, they are *compulsive*; they become fixated or focused on certain objects or behaviors, and *have* to have them, no matter what. Third, they become *emotionally labile*, and have sudden and unpredictable mood swings. Fourth, they exhibit *impaired judgment*.

So cortical hypofrontality, or shrinkage of the frontal lobes, causes these four behaviors, and they can result from a car wreck or from addiction.

A study on cocaine addiction published in 2002 shows volume loss, or shrinkage, in several areas of the brain, particularly the frontal control areas. A study from 2004 shows very similar results for methamphetamine. But we expect drugs to damage the brain, so these studies don't really surprise us.

Consider, though, a natural addiction, such as overeating leading to obesity. You might be surprised to learn that a study published in 2006 showed shrinkage in the frontal lobes in obesity very similar to that found in the cocaine and methamphetamine studies. And a study published in 2007 of persons exhibiting severe sexual addiction produced almost identical results to the cocaine, methamphetamine, and obesity studies. (Encouragingly, two studies, one on drug addiction [methamphetamine] and one on natural addiction [obesity] also show a return to more normal frontal lobe volumes with time in recovery.)

So we have four studies, two drug and two natural addiction studies, all done in different academic institutions by different research teams, and published over a five-year period in four different peer-reviewed scientific journals. And all four studies show that addictions physically affect the frontal lobes of the brain.

Pornography Addiction Causes Measurable Brain Damage

I mentioned that the dopamine systems don't work well in addiction, that they become damaged. This damage, as well as frontal lobe damage, can be shown with brain scans, such as functional MRI [magnetic resonance imaging], PET [positron emission tomography], and SPECT [single photon emission computed tomography] scans. Recent brain scan studies have not only shown abnormalities in cases of cocaine addiction, but also in cases of pathologic gambling and overeating leading to obesity.

So non-biased science is telling us that addiction is present when there is continued destructive behavior in spite of adverse consequences. As stated in the journal *Science*, "as far as the brain is concerned, a reward's a reward, regardless of whether it comes from a chemical or an experience."

What about pornography and sexual addiction? Dr. Eric Nestler, head of neuroscience research of Mount Sinai [Hospital] in New York and one of the most respected addiction scientists in the world, published a paper in the journal *Nature Neuroscience* in 2005 titled "Is There a Common Molecular Pathway for Addiction?" In this paper he said that the dopamine reward systems mediate not only drug addiction, but also "natural addictions (that is, compulsive consumption of natural rewards) such as pathological overeating, pathological gambling, and sexual addictions."

The prestigious Royal Society of London, founded in the 1660s, publishes the longest-running scientific journal in the world, *Philosophical Transactions of the Royal Society*. A recent issue devoted 17 articles to the current understanding of addiction. Interestingly, two of the articles were specifically concerned with natural addiction, pathologic gambling and overeating.

"Frantic Learning" and Porn Addiction

Drs. Robert Malenka and Julie Kauer, in a landmark paper in *Nature* in 2007 on mechanisms of the physical and chemical changes that occur in the brain cells of addicted individuals, said, "Addiction represents a pathological, yet powerful form of learning and memory." We now call these changes in brain cells "long term potentiation" and "long term depression," and speak of the brain as being plastic, or subject to change and rewiring.

Dr. Norman Doidge, a neurologist . . . , in his book *The Brain That Changes Itself*, describes how pornography causes rewiring of the neural circuits. He notes that in a study of men viewing Internet pornography, the men looked "uncannily" like rats pushing the lever to receive cocaine in the experimental [B.F.] Skinner boxes. Like the addicted rats, the men were desperately seeking the next fix, clicking the mouse just as the rats pushed the lever.

Pornography addiction is *frantic* learning, and perhaps this is why many who have struggled with multiple addictions report that it was the hardest for them to overcome. Drug addictions, while powerful, are more passive in a "thinking" kind of way, whereas pornography viewing, especially on the Internet, is a much more active process neurologically. The constant searching for and evaluating of each image or video clip for its potency and effect is an exercise in neuronal learning, limited only by the progressively rewired brain. Curiosities are thus fused into compulsions, and the need for a larger dopamine fix can drive the person from soft-core to hard-core to child pornography—and worse. A paper published in the

Journal of Family Violence in 2009 revealed that 85 percent of men arrested for child pornography had also physically abused children.

Brain Hormones, Porn Addiction, and Dehumanized Sexuality

In addition to cortical hypofrontality and downgrading of the mesolimbic dopaminergic systems, a third element appears to be important in pornography and sexual addiction. Oxytocin and vasopressin are important hormones in the brain with regard to physically performing sexually. Studies show that oxytocin is also important in increasing trust in humans, in emotional bonding between sexual mates, and in parental bonding. We are wired to bond to the object of our sexuality.

It is a good thing when this bonding occurs in a committed marriage relationship, but there is a dark side. When sexual gratification occurs in the context of pornography use, it can result in the formation of a virtual mistress of sorts. Dr. Victor Cline, in his essay, "Pornography's Effects on Adult and Child," describes this process as follows:

> In my experience as a sexual therapist, any individual who regularly masturbates to pornography is at risk of becoming, in time, a sexual addict, as well as conditioning himself into having a sexual deviancy and/or disturbing a bonded relationship with a spouse or girlfriend.

> A frequent side effect is that it also dramatically reduces their capacity to love (e.g., it results in a marked dissociation of sex from friendship, affection, caring, and other normal healthy emotions and traits which help marital relationships). Their sexual side becomes in a sense dehumanized. Many of them develop an "alien ego state" (or dark side), whose core is antisocial lust devoid of most values.

In time, the "high" obtained from masturbating to pornography becomes more important than real-life relationships. . . .

The process of masturbatory conditioning is inexorable and does not spontaneously remiss. The course of this illness may be slow and is nearly always hidden from view. It is usually a secret part of the man's life, and like a cancer, it keeps growing and spreading. It rarely ever reverses itself, and it is also very difficult to treat and heal. Denial on the part of the male addict and refusal to confront the problem are typical and predictable, and this almost always leads to marital or couple disharmony, sometimes divorce and sometimes the breaking up of other intimate relationships.

Dr. Doidge notes, "Pornographers promise healthy pleasure and a release from sexual tension, but what they often deliver is addiction, and an eventual decrease in pleasure. Paradoxically, the male patients I worked with often craved pornography but didn't like it." In the book *Pornified*, Pamela Paul gives numerous examples of this, and describes one person who decided to limit his pornography use, not from a moralist or guilt-based perspective, but out of a desire to again experience pleasure in actual physical relationships with women. . . .

The Triple Hook of Porn Addiction

Let me use a fishing analogy to illustrate some of these concepts. Every August, if possible, I try to be on the Unalakleet River in Alaska fishing for silver salmon. We use a particular lure, a triple hook called the Blue Fox pixie. As fishermen know, it is important to keep the drag loose just after hooking the fish, when it still has a lot of fight. As the fish tires, though, we tighten the drag and increase the resistance. In this way the fish is reeled into the boat and netted.

Similarly, pornography is a triple hook, consisting of cortical hypofrontality, dopaminergic downgrading, and oxytocin/

vasopressin bonding. Each of these hooks is powerful, and they are synergistic. Pornography sets its hooks very quickly and deeply, and as the addiction progresses, it progressively tightens the dopamine drag until there is no more play in the line. The person is drawn ever closer to the boat, and the waiting net.

Why is it essential to understand the addictive nature of pornography? Because if we view it as merely a bad habit, and do not afford those seeking healing the full support needed to overcome any true addiction, we will continue to be disappointed, as individuals and as a society. Pornography is the fabric used to weave a tapestry of sexual permissiveness that undermines the very foundation of society. Biologically, it destroys the ability of a population to sustain itself. It is a demographic disaster.

It is interesting that food and gambling addiction don't create the same emotionally charged responses that discussions of pornography and sexual addiction invariably precipitate, despite convincing evidence that all three are "brain" addictions just like substance addictions. In August of 2010 the American Society of Addiction Medicine (ASAM) released its new definition of addiction, this after a process of over four years involving over 80 experts. In contrast to the American Psychological Association, ASAM comprises physicians who possess the ability to prescribe medication to treat both the psychological and physical effects of addiction and withdrawal. Significantly, the more biologically based ASAM now says addiction is a chronic disease of the brain involving the reward/motivation/memory systems. More importantly the definition states, for the first time, that addiction can include not just substances such as cocaine and opioids, but also behaviors such as sex, food, and gambling. In other words, it is more about the end process in the brain than the substance or behavior.

> *"Since most of us regularly engage in many [pleasurable] activities in our daily lives, but nevertheless fail to become addicted to them, there has to be something more to it besides the dopamine rush."*

Pornography Is Not Addictive

Cristian C.A. Bodo

Cristian C.A. Bodo is a neuroscientist whose research largely focuses on the hormonal regulation of mammalian sexual behavior. In the following viewpoint, Bodo discusses the development of our modern notion of "addiction" as it relates to the pleasure mechanisms of the human brain. While he acknowledges that the stimulation experienced while viewing and masturbating to pornography may be neurochemically indistinguishable from the stimulation provided by addictive substances like cocaine, it is likewise indistinguishable from the stimulation of scoring a goal in a soccer match or riding a roller coaster—activities not generally considered addictive, or even "habit forming."

As you read, consider the following questions:

1. What did Freud identify as the "primary addiction"? By modern standards, were people of his era very knowledgeable about the structures and function of the human brain?

2. The author identifies two groups of people who might be especially eager to have a compulsive interest in pornography accepted as a form of recognized addiction; who are these two groups of people?

3. If injecting cocaine, dancing, watching TV, and viewing pornography are all pleasurable because of the same brain circuitry, why are some activities addictive to some people and not to others, according to Bodo?

Things used to be pretty straightforward: You were involved in a stable and fulfilling long-term relationship, but nevertheless the temptations were many and practicing strict monogamy proved way too hard. Eventually, you were caught and you had to decide whether to call it quits or to go back to your partner, admit your full responsibility, beg for forgiveness, and promise that it was never going to happen again. Nowadays, however, there may be a third option: You can claim that you are a victim of sexual addiction, simply unable to manage your sexual urges despite what you know is best for you.

Defining Addiction

This term has been steadily gaining recognition among the public, helped by several high-profile cases of celebrities who checked themselves into "sex addiction rehab" after their infidelities were made public. Self-help groups such as Sex Addicts Anonymous and Sexaholics Anonymous have sprung up in the last few decades, following the 12-step system first made popular by Alcoholics Anonymous. There is even a proliferation of fictional characters from recent movies, novels, and TV series who are described as sex addicts and regularly attend meetings organized by these kinds of groups. The proponents of the concept routinely argue that sexual addiction and substance addiction are analogous syndromes, with both of them rendering the individual a slave to a particular source of gratification at the expense of everything else in his/her life. But is there strong scientific evidence supporting a common physiological basis between these versions of compulsive behavior?

The answer depends strongly in the definition of "addiction" that we choose to adopt, and this is by no means a trivial matter. Originally, addiction was a term coined to describe a psychological disorder ([Sigmund] Freud himself refers to compulsive masturbation as the primary addiction in his writings). Granted, in those days modern neuroscience did not yet exist, and therefore the workings of the mind tended to be considered in isolation of brain physiology, simply because very little was known about the latter. The focus gradually shifted in the course of the twentieth century, as scientists started investigating the changes that substances of abuse provoked in patterns of neuronal firing and neurotransmitter release. This led to the description of the mesolimbic reward system: essentially a group of neurons that release dopamine into a specific brain area (the nucleus accumbens) in response to pleasurable stimuli. In fact, it was discovered that what made these stimuli pleasurable was precisely this focalized release of dopamine, and that certain drugs had the ability to stimulate this system even in their absence. Addiction was thus redefined in terms of the neurochemistry of the brain. Any substance and/or stimulus that was capable of overstimulating the system normally responsible for our experience of pleasure was in principle potentially addictive. Notice, however, that since the great majority of us (except perhaps those with severe cases of anhedonia [inability to feel pleasure]) experience pleasure regularly in our daily lives, the difference between a normal, well-adjusted individual and an addict becomes, under this new definition, only a matter of degree. We all experience dopamine highs routinely, but the addict lives for them.

Since drugs of abuse were only "hijacking" our internal pleasure system, there was no longer any need to restrict the list of stimuli capable of becoming addictive. Why not include also behavioral patterns like eating, gambling, shopping, working, running, using electronic devices, playing video games . . . or having sex? After all, sex is one of the first things that comes to mind when prompted to name a pleasurable experience. Thus, behavioral addictions began to be included in medical manuals, and terms like sex addiction were incorporated into pop culture. It is interesting to remark, however, that since most of us regularly engage in many of these activities in our daily lives, but nevertheless fail to become addicted to them, there has to be something more to it besides the dopamine rush.

The Argument for Addictive Sex

There have been attempts to take this even further. In July 2005 the British newspaper the *Guardian* ran a piece on the research of Dr. Judith Reisman, who published an article entitled "The Psychopharmacology of Pictorial Pornography: Restructuring Brain, Mind & Memory & Subverting Freedom of Speech." In it, Reisman characterizes pornography as an "erototoxin that produces an addictive drug cocktail of testosterone, oxytocin, dopamine and serotonin with a measurable organic effect on the brain." She admits that one of her objectives is to demonstrate that pornography restructures the brain of those who consume it much in the same way as drugs of abuse often act to generate dependence. This will in turn open the door to potential lawsuits against the providers of pornography, in the same line as those brought against big tobacco companies and fast-food chains.

The *Spectator*, a weekly British magazine known for its conservative slant, ran a piece some years ago on the story of Sean Thomas, a man who confessed falling victim to "Internet porn addiction." Thomas detailed how he went from an initial attitude of indifference to an ever-increasing interest to explore complex sexual scenarios on display in pornographic sites, how this led to sleep deprivation and health deterioration, and how this ended up landing him in the ER. (At this point he decided to assume himself as an addict, only to discover later that many of his male friends also identified with this general behavioral pattern.) In a recently published book on brain plasticity, its author, Norman Doidge, writes, "The men at their computers looking at porn were uncannily like the rats in the cages of the National Institutes of Health (NIH), pressing the bar to get a shot of dopamine or its equivalent. Though they didn't know it, they had been seduced into pornographic training sessions that met all the conditions required for plastic change of brain maps. Each time they felt sexual excitement and had an orgasm when they masturbated, a spritz of dopamine, the reward neurotransmitter, consolidated the connections made in the brain during the sessions."

Addiction Is More than a Spritz of Dopamine

This kind of rhetoric brings to the table the specious issue of free will of the individual. Remarkably, the same sort of arguments can be used for two different purposes that at first appear as diametrically opposed. On the one hand, individuals themselves can use them to avoid having to take responsibility for their own behavior ("I just couldn't help doing it, I have an addict brain"). On the other hand, they can be used to single out certain types of behavior deemed as undesirable or pernicious by a particular group, argue that they modify the neurochemistry of the brain so that individuals who engage in them regularly become addicts, and use this as an argument to justify their banishment. As Dr. Reisman put it rather bluntly in her testimony for a hearing held by the U.S. Senate on the subject, "Thanks to the latest advances in neuroscience, we now know that pornographic visual images imprint and alter the brain, triggering an instant, involuntary, but lasting, biochemical memory trail, arguably, subverting the First Amendment by overriding the cognitive speech process."

The scientific basis to support such arguments is, however, very scant. On one end of the spectrum, it is widely accepted that certain substances such as opioids do indeed trigger long-lasting changes in the organism of individuals who consume them regularly. This becomes evident when these individuals experience physical symptoms of withdrawal, including sweating, nausea, fatigue, vomiting, and pain. In these cases, the body of the addict has become used to the presence of the substance, and when it is not there anymore, it can no longer function properly. But beyond these clear-cut cases, defining addiction from a neurological standpoint becomes more and more difficult. Sure enough, both shooting cocaine and having an orgasm stimulate your mesolimbic system by a sudden release of dopamine, but so does scoring a goal in a soccer game, going on a roller-coaster ride, skiing, diving, dancing, or watching a movie. In fact, it may be argued that every single action that we can describe as pleasurable involves the activation of this system. But if we can potentially become addicted to anything (or anything pleasurable, at least), where exactly do we draw the line between healthy pleasure-seeking and addiction? Moreover, it goes without saying that most people regularly engage in some form of sexual activity (or in drinking or TV-watching, for that matter) without it becoming disruptive of their occupational, domestic, or social obligations. Simple stimulation of the pleasure centers in the brain cannot then be the entire explanation. Somehow those who fall victim to an addiction are unable to resist impulses to engage in a specified behavior, no matter how inconvenient this may become beyond a certain limit, whereas the non-addicted does not seem to have a problem overruling these impulses when the circumstances call for it.

Using Science to Legitimize Social Control

Whether this reflects an underlying difference in the way the brain works is still hotly debated between scientists working in the field of addiction, and no clear consensus has been reached yet. The same goes for the origin of these differences, in case they happen to exist at all. Are they genetic? Do they reflect exposure to a particular environment during early life? And if so, which kinds of stimuli are likely to lead to the development of a personality prone to become addicted, and when do they have their effect? Given that the actual number of research groups around the world that are currently looking to find answers to these questions is enormous, we may expect to have a much clearer picture of addiction as a biological phenomenon a few decades, or even a few years, down the road. In the meantime, it is important to bear in mind that scientific explanations are often used to legitimize arguments from those who have social control as their hidden agenda.

> *"It is a growing problem that has re-*
> *sulted in child pornography charges be-*
> *ing filed against some teens. . . . But*
> *. . . 'sexting' is about more than possi-*
> *bly criminal activity: It's about life and*
> *death."*

Her Teen Committed Suicide over "Sexting"

Mike Celizic

Mike Celizic was a noted journalist and sports writer. For many years, he wrote a column for MSNBC.com. In the following viewpoint, he shares the sad case of Jesse Logan. In 2008 Logan committed suicide after sexually explicit images she had taken of herself and sent to a boyfriend—this practice often called "sexting"—began circulating around her school. Although Logan sought to use her experience to warn other teens of the dangers—both legal and psycho-emotional—associated with sexting, she was ultimately overwhelmed by the ceaseless bullying and social exclusion.

As you read, consider the following questions:

1. What percentage of teens have sent sexually explicit text messages? What percentage have received such messages?

2. What laws can apply to sexting, according to Parry Aftab?

3. What percentage of boys claim to have seen sexual images of female classmates? What percentage indicate they share such images after breaking up with a girl?

The image was blurred and the voice distorted, but the words spoken by a young Ohio woman are haunting. She had sent nude pictures of herself to a boyfriend. When they broke up, he sent them to other high school girls. The girls were harassing her, calling her a slut and a whore. She was miserable and depressed, afraid even to go to school.

And now Jesse Logan was going on a Cincinnati television station to tell her story. Her purpose was simple: "I just want to make sure no one else will have to go through this again."

The interview was in May 2008. Two months later, Jessica Logan hanged herself in her bedroom. She was 18.

Conveying the Message

"She was vivacious. She was fun. She was artistic. She was compassionate. She was a good kid," the young woman's mother, Cynthia Logan, told *Today*'s Matt Lauer Friday in New York. Still grieving over the loss of her daughter, she said she is taking her story public to warn kids about the dangers of sending sexually charged pictures and messages to boyfriends and girlfriends.

"It's very, very difficult. She's my only child," Logan told Lauer. "I'm trying my best to get the message out there."

It is a growing problem that has resulted in child pornography charges being filed against some teens across the nation.

But for Cynthia Logan, "sexting" is about more than possibly criminal activity: It's about life and death.

Last fall, the National Campaign to Prevent Teen and Unplanned Pregnancy surveyed teens and young adults about sexting—sending sexually charged material via cell phone text messages—or posting such materials online. The results revealed that 39 percent of teens are sending or posting sexually suggestive messages, and 48 percent reported receiving such messages.

'She Was Being Tortured'

Jesse Logan's mother said she never knew the full extent of her daughter's anguish until it was too late. Cynthia Logan only learned there was a problem at all when she started getting daily letters from her daughter's school reporting that the young woman was skipping school.

"I only had snapshots, bits and pieces, until the very last semester of school," Logan told Lauer.

She took away her daughter's car and drove her to school herself, but Jesse still skipped classes. She told her mother there were pictures involved and that a group of younger girls who had received them were harassing her, calling her vicious names, even throwing objects at her. But she didn't realize the full extent of her daughter's despair.

"She was being attacked and tortured," Logan said.

"When she would come to school, she would always hear, 'Oh, that's the girl who sent the picture. She's just a whore,'" Jesse's friend, Lauren Taylor, told NBC News.

Logan said that officials at Sycamore High School were aware of the harassment but did not take sufficient action to stop it. She said that a school official offered only to go to one of the girls who had the pictures and tell her to delete them from her phone and never speak to Jesse again. That girl was 16.

Why the Government Must Treat Sexting as Child Pornography

The reasonable expectation that the material will ultimately be disseminated is by itself a compelling state interest for preventing the production of this material. In addition, the statute was intended to protect minors ... from their own lack of judgment. . . .

[Minors are] simply too young to make an intelligent decision about engaging in sexual conduct and memorializing it. Mere production of these videos or pictures may also result in psychological trauma to the teenagers involved.

Further, if these pictures are ultimately released, future damage may be done to these minors' careers or personal lives. These children are not mature enough to make rational decisions concerning all the possible negative implications of producing these videos.

Not only can [their] computers be hacked, but by transferring the photos using the net, the photos may have been and perhaps still are accessible to the provider and/or other individuals. Computers also allow for long-term storage of information which may then be disseminated at some later date. The state has a compelling interest in seeing that material which will have such negative consequences is never produced.

James Wolf, Majority Opinion, A.H., a Child, Appellant vs. State of Florida, Appellee, *Case no. 1D06-0162 (Florida District Court of Appeals, First District), 2007.*

Logan suggested talking to the parents of the girls who were bullying Jesse, but her daughter said that would only open her to even more ridicule.

"She said, 'No, I need to do something else. I'm going to go on the news,' and that's what she did," Logan said.

Finding Jesse

When Cynthia Logan decided to go public with her story, she told Lauer that a school official told a local television station that he had given Jesse the option of prosecuting her tormentors. "That was not so. It's absolutely not true," she told Lauer. "And if he did, why didn't I get a notice in the mail that he gave her that option?"

After her daughter's death, Logan quit her job and was hospitalized for a time with what she described as a mental breakdown. When she spoke about finding her daughter in her bedroom last July, tears coursed down her cheeks.

Jesse had been talking about going to the University of Cincinnati to study graphic design. Her mother thought she was over the worst of the bullying. Then one of Jesse's acquaintances committed suicide. Jesse went to the funeral. When she came home, she hanged herself.

"I just had a scan of the room, her closet doors were open," Logan told NBC News. "And I walked over into her room and saw her hanging. The cell phone was in the middle of the floor."

Quest for Justice

Logan said she's been through six lawyers in what has so far been an unsuccessful battle to hold school officials responsible for the bullying of her daughter.

She was joined on *Today* by Parry Aftab, an Internet security expert and activist in the battle to protect teens from the dangers that lurk in cyberspace. Aftab said that there are laws that apply.

"There absolutely is a law," Aftab told Lauer. "It depends on the age of the child. If somebody's under the age of 18, it's child pornography, and even the girl that posted the pictures can be charged. They could be registered sex offenders at the end of all of this. Even at the age of 18, because it was sent to somebody under age, it's disseminating pornography to a minor. There are criminal charges that could be made here."

Aftab said that it is normal kids just like Jesse who fall victim to the perils of the Internet and the easy exchange of information on cell phones.

"We talked about her being a good kid, a normal kid. Those are most of the ones that are sending out those images," she said. "Forty-four percent of the boys say that they've seen sexual images of girls in their school, and about 15 percent of them are disseminating those images when they break up with the girls."

Aftab asked Logan to join her in her fight against the electronic exploitation of kids. "I'm going to get her involved in a huge campaign to allow kids to understand the consequences of this and allow schools to understand what they need to do to keep our kids alive," she said.

Aftab turned to Logan to see if she would help.

"Absolutely," she said.

"Many, especially legal experts, are disturbed by the fact that a healthy horndog of a teenager could be grouped in the same criminal category as a clinically ill pedophile."

Sexting Is a Normal Part of Teen Sexuality, Not Pornography

Tracy Clark-Flory

Tracy Clark-Flory is a staff writer for Salon.com. Her essay "In Defense of Casual Sex" appeared in the Best Sex Writing 2009 *anthology. In the following viewpoint, the author discusses recent sexting cases, in which teenagers sent nude or seminude photographs via text messaging, that have led to child pornography charges against both the recipients of the images and against their creators—even though the creators of those images were the same teenage girls who were the "victims" of the crime. Clark-Flory indicates that this contradiction is not just confusing but greatly concerns both sex educators and legal scholars, who find these prosecutions to be as hurtful as they are nonsensical.*

As you read, consider the following questions:

1. According to the author, if a minor creates a sexually explicit image of herself and never shows it to anyone— either accidentally or purposefully—is that image considered child pornography under the law?

2. According to the poll cited by the author, what percentage of teens have shared nude or seminude photos or videos of themselves? With whom have they mostly shared these?

3. New York University law professor Amy Adler indicates that child pornography law was conceived under a certain notion of how child pornography is created. How does sexting differ from the traumatic process that leads to traditional child pornography?

The photographs show three naked underage girls posing lasciviously for the camera. The perps [perpetrators] who took the pictures were busted in Greensburg, Pa., and charged with manufacturing, disseminating and possessing child pornography—and so were their subjects. That's because they are one and the same.

Child or Child Pornography

It all started when the girls, ages 14 and 15, decided to take nudie cell phone snapshots of themselves. Then, maybe feeling dizzy from the rush of wielding their feminine wiles, the trio text messaged the photos to some friends at Greensburg Salem High School. When one of the students' cell phones was confiscated at school, the photos were discovered. Police opened an investigation and, in addition to the girls' being indicted as kiddie pornographers, three boys who received the pictures were slammed with charges of child porn possession. All but one ultimately accepted lesser misdemeanor charges.

"Sexting," where kids trade X-rated pictures via text message, has made headlines recently after a rash of cases in which child pornography charges have been brought not against dangerous pedophiles but hormonally haywire teenagers—potentially leaving them branded sex offenders for life. Just last week [in February 2009], there came news that a middle-school boy in Falmouth, Mass., might face child porn charges for sending a naughty photo of his 13-year-old girlfriend to five buddies, who are also being investigated. There's been plenty of outrage to go around: Some parents are angry to see teens criminalized for simply being sexual, while others find the raunchy shots pornographic, another blinking neon sign of moral decay in a "Girls Gone Wild" era. In both cases, it amounts to a tug-of-war between teenagers' entitled sense of sexual autonomy and society's desire to protect them.

It's rather stunning that in the same age of the Pussycat Dolls, Disney starlets' sexy photo scandals, Slut-o-ween costumes for kids and preteen push-up bras and thongs, teenagers are being charged with child porn possession for having photographs of their own naked bodies. That noise you hear? It's the grating sound of cultural dissonance.

Testing the Waters of Sexuality in a New Era

According to these recent interpretations of the law, a curious teenage girl who embarks on an *Our Bodies, Ourselves* journey of vaginal self-discovery, and simply replaces a hand mirror with a digital camera, is a kiddie pornographer. The same goes for the boy who memorializes his raging boner or the post-pubescent girl who takes test shots of herself practicing the porn star poses she has studied online. Theoretically, this is true regardless of whether they share the pictures with anyone, and if they do share them, they could be additionally charged with peddling child porn.

There are plenty of examples of the moral and legal gray areas created as technology broadens our behaviors:

cyber-cheating, MySpace bullying, online gossip, upskirting, employers' Web snooping. When it comes to "sexting," though, the potentially damaging implications—for child pornography law, free speech and kids' sexuality—are abundant. And it's not going away anytime soon. A recent online poll found that 20 percent of teens have shared nude or seminude photos or videos of themselves, the majority with a boyfriend or girl-friend. (Sure, voluntary polls tend to be self-selecting, but the results seem obvious, maybe even understated.) Teens will, as they always have, experiment with their sexuality. But at a time when free hard-core porn is ubiquitous, technology is cheap and the Internet is a comfortable channel for expression and experimentation, is it really any surprise that this is a generation of amateur pornographers?

It certainly isn't to 20-somethings like myself who came of age during the Internet's youth. By the time I was 14, I had seen my share of online porn and late-night HBO and made frequent use of the phrase "U wanna cyber?" in early AOL chat rooms. In high school in Berkeley, Calif., at least two stu-dent sex tapes were rumored to be making the rounds. I didn't have a cell phone camera or a webcam, thank god—though I did have a Polaroid camera, which, to be sure, my longtime boyfriend and I toyed around with.

This is all part of how kids initiate themselves into our sexual culture long before they actually have sex. At one time, that meant a boy would flip through his father's stash of *Play-boys* and a girl would try on her mother's ample bra. For me, it meant privately mimicking the stripper moves I had seen on TV and having online chats with people who occasionally turned out to be aging pens. It was the best way I knew to try on, test out and confirm my femininity without actually hav-ing sex. (And that's having been raised by hippie parents who compared the spiritual magic of sex to "two star systems col-liding in outer space.")

Chan Lowe, "Sexting," *Sun Sentinel*, February 5, 2009.

A Different Perspective on Technology

That sexual rite of passage remains, but today's teens have an entirely different notion of privacy than past generations. They grew up in the exhibitionistic Web culture of LiveJournal, YouTube and MySpace. They've seen girls on TV playfully jiggling their breasts for plastic beads, *Real World* cast members boldly screwing in front of cameras, Britney [Spears] flashing her bald lady parts. These days, why would a girl be concerned about her silly topless snapshot circulating around school?

That's certainly the case with 16-year-old Melissa, a student at a high school near Greensburg Salem, who has never worried about any of the X-rated pictures she's shared, because she cropped her face out of the photos, so "no one could identify me unless like [they] lifted up my shirt to figure it out haha," she wrote in a message sent on the blog platform Xanga. On her profile page, a rap song with the lyrics "I jus' wanna act like a porno flick actor" plays. It also exhibits a self-portrait she took with a cell phone camera of her reflection in a floor-length mirror; the sassy expression on her face matches the page's background: a sexy hot pink and lime green leopard print.

Joey, an 18-year-old who graduated from a San Francisco high school last year, has gotten X-rated snapshots from girls on his phone, through e-mail and on his MySpace page since he was 15. Some were longtime girlfriends that he swapped photos with and others were girls he'd just casually met; some pictures were suggestive, others were explicit. . . .

Sexting Teens Are Not the Real Threat

"Older adults have a short memory. There were things we did—people flashed each other and played spin the bottle," says Elizabeth Schroeder, director of Answer, Rutgers University's program dedicated to promoting sexuality education. "This is this generation's way of doing that." Heather Corinna, the 38-year-old founder of Scarleteen, a Web site that provides sex-positive education for young adults, agrees: "Before we had this media, we had video cameras, before that film cameras, before that the written word, and all throughout, public or semipublic sex, ways of proclaiming to peers that one is sexually active or available to become so," she says.

But, clearly, there is a big difference between testifying on the wall of the boys' bathroom about the toe-curling blow jobs the school's head cheerleader gives and sending your buddies photographic proof. These digital offerings bring the potential for humiliation and blackmail if the photos or video get into the wrong hands—and, let's face it, they often do. Acting as your girlfriend's personal porno star is one thing; ending up a pedophile's favorite child pinup is quite another.

There's good reason to be concerned about teens being self-pornographers. But many, especially legal experts, are disturbed by the fact that a healthy horndog of a teenager could be grouped in the same criminal category as a clinically ill pedophile. "These cases are picturing these teenagers as both predators and victims of themselves," says Amy Adler, a law professor at New York University who has studied child porn laws. "Child porn law was founded on a very different vision of what the major threat was."

That major threat, of course, is supposed to be adults who produce and peddle child smut. Reed Lee, a Chicago attorney and board member of the Free Speech Coalition, says: "A law to protect victims shouldn't send those very victims to jail."

A Normal Teenage Experience

Typically, kiddie porn is seen as exponentially harmful because it's more than the original sexual abuse: It allows for a reliving of the trauma every time another pervert gets ahold of the material. But "if the initial photograph was not taken as part of a traumatic episode and was, like it or not, part of a more normal teenage experience, the abuse rationale becomes harder to see," Adler argues. Still, plenty of child pornography cases have been prosecuted where the original photo is awfully benign—for example, a family picture taken at a nudist camp that is discovered by a pedophile and then cropped to reveal only the naked kid.

But it's tough to impress those kinds of nuances on kids, says Los Angeles criminal defense attorney Jeffrey Douglas. He once spoke to a high school class and tried to explain that, even though everyone seems to be "sexting," it "can literally destroy your life." The response? A boy rolled his eyes while making a grand jack-off gesture. "It's just the bullshit that adults tell them when they come to talk to them," he said. "It's tragically funny."

Douglas points out that the bungled law reveals fascinating cultural conflicts about childhood and teen sexuality. "I think the problem originates from the pathological fear that our culture, particularly the legal part of the culture, takes toward juvenile sexuality." He has defended numerous child porn cases and says prosecutors will treat the exchange of trial evidence like "an undercover heroin deal." Douglas says, "The fear is so enormous that it's like you're dealing with something radioactive. They don't consider the context or the meaning."

The context here is that teens are undertaking the sexploration that our porned culture at once dictates and forbids—in the same way that girls are taught that there is desirable validation in their sexuality and then are shamed for actually being sexual. Rutgers' Elizabeth Schroeder says an example of this contradiction is that sex educators like herself have to fight an uphill battle just to get into schools, while all it takes is a click of a button and a kid can catch an episode of *G String Divas*. She once asked a group of 12-year-old boys what they thought it meant to be a girl and the first response was: "Girls are here to give lap dances to boys."

> *"Should we allow the state to force chil-dren ... to attend a session espousing the views of one particular government official on what it means to be a girl?"*

Sexting Prosecution Unfairly Targets Young Women

Christopher Keelty

Christopher Keelty is a writer living in Philadelphia, where he works for the American Civil Liberties Union (ACLU). In the following viewpoint, he recounts the ACLU's defense of three teenage girls living in Tunkhannock, a small, rural town in Wyoming County, Pennsylvania. In 2008 the teachers at Tunkhannock High School discovered pictures of nineteen female students circulating on student cell phones. Although few of the pictures featured nudity and none depicted sexual activity, Wyoming County district attorney George Skumanick Jr. considered them child pornography and moved forward with punishing the girls.

As you read, consider the following questions:

1. What were the two options Wyoming County, PA, dis-trict attorney George Skumanick Jr. offered the teen girls who had appeared in "provocative" cell phone pictures?

2. Could a girl living in Wyoming County, PA, be prosecuted for being photographed while wearing a bikini?

3. How many boys did Skumanick charge with distribution of child pornography? Why?

On January 15, [2010] the U.S. Court of Appeals for the Third Circuit heard arguments in *Miller, et al. v. Skumanick*, a child pornography case that, oddly, involves no child pornography. The case goes back to 2006, when two girls aged 12 were photographed by another friend on her digital camera. The two girls were depicted from the waist up, wearing bras. In a separate situation, our third client was photographed as she emerged from the shower, with a towel wrapped around her waist and the upper body exposed. Neither of the photos depicted genitalia or any sexual activity or context. In 2008 the girls' school district learned that these and other photos were circulating, confiscated several students' cell phones, and turned the photos in question over to the Wyoming County district attorney, George Skumanick Jr.

An Ultimatum: Reeducation or Prosecution

Skumanick sent a letter to the girls and their parents, offering an ultimatum. They could attend a five-week reeducation program of his own design, which included topics like "what it means to be a girl in today's society" and "non-traditional societal and job roles." They would also be placed on probation, subjected to random drug testing, and required to write essays explaining how their actions were wrong. If the girls refused the program, the letter explained, the girls would be charged with felony child pornography, a charge that carries a possible 10-year prison sentence.

Nineteen families received these letters. Sixteen consented to reeducation. Three decided their girls would benefit more from a lesson in constitutional law than from Skumanick's views on "'what it means to be a girl in today's society,'" and called the ACLU [American Civil Liberties Union] of Pennsylvania. In March 2009, a federal judge granted a temporary restraining order preventing Mr. Skumanick and the Wyoming County, Pa., district attorney's office from going ahead with any prosecution. Now it falls to the Court of Appeals to decide whether the DA's office (Skumanick lost his bid for reelection in November) can proceed with prosecution.[1]

This case has been branded as the "'Sexting Case,'" and headlines ask questions like "'Sexting: Child porn or child's play?'" But this case has nothing to do with sex, and nothing to do with pornography. This is a case of a government official using the law to force his personal morals on others. Last February [2009], Skumanick told a group of students and parents that he had the authority to prosecute a girl for being photographed in a bikini on a beach, because the photo was "provocative." In their brief to the Third Circuit, the DA's office asserts their opinion that no person could exchange such photographs for any other reason except sexual gratification. Their attorney reasserted this right before the court, stating that a minor's transmission of any photograph of herself containing any nudity is never protected under the First Amendment.

Legally Enforcing One Man's Morality

Even if the photographs in question could be construed as pornographic, Skumanick lacked any evidence that the girls had transmitted the photos. His only basis for probable cause, in the words of their attorney, was "'the presence of [those] photographs on the cell phones of [their] classmates.'" It was this lack of probable cause that led to the initial restraining order.

Interestingly, none of the classmates who distributed the photos received letters from Skumanick. Only the girls who

---

1. On March 17, 2010, the Third Circuit Court of Appeals ruled that the girls could not be charged or prosecuted.

The View of a Defendant in the Pennsylvania Sexting Case

As the 17-year-old who took seminude self-portraits waited in line [to view the photos involved in the case], she realized that [District Attorney George] Skumanick and other investigators had viewed the pictures. When the adults began to crowd around Mr. Skumanick, the 17-year-old worried they could see her photo and recalls she said, "I think the worst punishment is knowing that all you old guys saw me naked. I just think you guys are all just perverts."

Dionne Searcey,
"A Lawyer, Some Teens and a Fight Over 'Sexting,'"
Wall Street Journal, *April 21, 2009.*

appeared in the photos were threatened with child porn charges. If the DA did in fact regard these photos as pornographic, why not file distribution charges against the boys? A clue may be found in their argument before the Third Circuit. In narrating the case, their attorney explained how, after the girls were photographed, "high school boys did as high school boys will do, and traded the photos among themselves."

Ultimately, that's what this case comes down to: one man's view on how a young woman should conduct herself. The boys who traded the photos bear no responsibility and require no reeducation. Instead the girls are threatened with felony charges and lifelong registration as sex offenders. To apply such a penalty, designed to protect minors against exploitation, is a grotesque misapplication—and that's once again assuming that the photographs in question could possibly be construed as pornographic. In reality, there was no way such charges would ever stick, and the DA's office had to know this.

The child porn charges were merely a threat, to force the parents to subject their children to Skumanick's moral view of the world, where any and all child nudity is illegal and bras and bikinis are pornographic.

What It Means to Be a Girl

Instead these parents asserted their constitutional right to dictate the upbringing of their children; their right to say "'we don't think this was wrong, and we're not forcing our children to put that in writing, and we're not forcing them to attend your reeducation session,'" without fear of retribution from the DA's office. It is certainly important, in this era of Facebook and Twitter and text messaging, that children learn the consequences of sharing digital photographs of themselves, but as ACLU of Pennsylvania legal director Witold Walczak puts it, "prosecutors should not be using heavy artillery like child-pornography charges to teach that lesson."

The DA's office argues that the federal court had no place issuing a restraining order, and that the proper procedure would have been to allow the prosecution to go forward and for the girls to mount a constitutional defense against the charges—but the prosecution itself was the threat. The agony of a felony prosecution, of hiring attorneys and mounting a defense, of the media attention surrounding the prosecution of a 16-year-old girl as a child pornographer were, in Walczak's words, "the Sword of Damacles," the threat of retribution if these parents refused to turn their children over to Skumanick.

The central question of this case was perhaps best framed by Judge Thomas L. Ambro during Third Circuit arguments: "Should we allow the state to force children, by threat of prosecution, to attend a session espousing the views of the particular government official on what it means to be a girl?"

> "A whole new set of outsiders [enjoy]
> ... a cheap, almost barrierless way to
> make, distribute, and sell videos of
> themselves having sex. ... [It is] a bur-
> geoning empire of lemonade-stand
> porn."

Online Pornography Creates a Unique Creative and Entrepreneurial Outlet for Individuals

Benjamin Wallace

Benjamin Wallace is a writer who has contributed articles to GQ, Details, Salon, *and the* Washington Post. *The following viewpoint is drawn from an essay exploring the universe of pornographic "tube sites." These are YouTube-like websites that stream porn, much of it without charge, freely mixing short clips released as promotional material by studios with pirated pornographic videos. Alongside this professionally produced content, many tube sites also make it possible for users to upload their own videos, and to earn money as others pay to view them.*

Wallace interviews several people who post content to such sites; many of them assert that creating and posting pornographic videos offers a creative and sexual outlet and enables them to earn a decent living.

As you read, consider the following questions:

1. How much does a LiveJasmin.com "camgirl" earn per minute spent talking with a paying client?

2. What reasons do Cole Maverick and Hunter cite for posting images and videos to XTube?

3. Of the amateur videos posted to XTube, what percentage are pay-per-view? What do the other individuals who post get out of sharing their sexually explicit images and videos?

The woman on my MacBook screen, whose username is xTattooSurprisex, has punky two-tone hair and wears a scoop-neck top that reveals her ample chest and a clavicle tattoo reading BEAUTIFUL DISASTER. I chose xTattooSurprisex for my "private chat" because she looked American. (Most of the girls on LiveJasmin.com, the biggest cam site, seem to be from Russia.) When I tell her I'm a journalist and just want to talk, Roxy, as she introduces herself, immediately types that she is camming "not by choice."

A Grim Story, but a Decent Living

Roxy moved to New Mexico from Washington State to get away from her alcoholic mother, who, she says, was stalking her and caused her to lose her job at the Cheesecake Factory. She's 20, and has been doing this since July. She says that she was going to lose her house if she didn't get a job, and the money's not bad. I'm paying LiveJasmin $1.99 per minute, of which Roxy receives about 70 cents. She tells me she might make $1,200 a month. She doesn't want to do this forever, but at times it can be fun, most of the guys are nice, and she just ignores the mean ones. Some of her orgasms are fake, she says, and some are real.

Unlike recorded porn, live cams are immune to piracy, which has made them especially successful as a business proposition. In this sense, the cams function as anti-tubes ["tubes" refer to YouTube-like sites], but the two technologies have together opened up an entirely new frottage industry, so to speak: a grassroots, DIY [do-it-yourself] porn democracy where anyone with a bedroom, a cam, and a web connection can set up as a one-woman or -man operation. LiveJasmin has some 40,000 registered cammers. "Today," porn distributor Farrell Timlake says, "cams are the closest thing to amateur."

When an "Amateur" Isn't an Amateur

"Amateur" is a semantically slippery term, as Timlake will tell you. A graduate of the Kent School in Connecticut, he spent a good deal of the early nineties submitting his own home sex tapes to Homegrown Video, which functioned as a kind of VHS video exchange for swingers. In 1992, he and his brother Moffitt . . . , bankrolled by their mother, bought out the company, which they run together and which has, so they plausibly claim, the largest library of amateur videos in the world. Since then, Farrell and Moffitt have watched "amateur" move from almost a fringe fetish to one of pornography's most popular aesthetics—and, as such, one co-opted by the pros.

Pretty much all the porn labeled "gonzo" and "reality" these days is a put-on, Timlake insists. In the *Dancing Bear* series, a male stripper wearing an enormous bear head performs for a bachelorette party until several fairly respectable-looking women suddenly lose control and start fellating him. "That stuff looks pretty real," he says. "It takes a minute, but where are there roomfuls of women willing to have sex with a guy?" Watch a few of them, and you'll notice the same women reappearing. Another series, *Dare Dorm*, claims to pay real college kids for tapes of campus orgies, but Timlake isn't buying it. "I can always tell, because most college kids can't afford as many tattoos as those people have." . . . A recent vogue for "ex-girlfriend porn"—purportedly uploaded by vengeful former boyfriends—democratizes the celebrity sex tape but is also phony (actual unauthorized home videos would pose legal risks to the hosting websites).

Making a Living in Amateur Online Porn

If you expand the idea of amateur, though, to encompass a whole new set of outsiders for whom cam sites and tubes have provided a cheap, almost barrierless way to make, distribute, and sell videos of themselves having sex, well, then, we're living in a grand age of micro-smut, a burgeoning empire of lemonade-stand porn. XTube, for instance, offers a mix of straight and gay movies, some of which are free, others pay-per-view. The majority of XTube's content was made by a professional studio, but the site's "amateur" section allows any of its visitors to upload content. A frequent uploader with the user name Tnhotbtm has been on the site for six months. "I enjoyed the videos I was viewing personally, so I decided to add my own," says Tnhotbtm, whose real name is Rob. "I never really liked mainstream porn. I always like guys that look like you could walk up and talk to them in a club, not the perfect shaved guys that never give you the time of day." Rob had dabbled in shooting his own, self-starring movies, and for the last ten years he had sold them as DVDs through his website atticmen.com or streamed through video-on-demand companies. Then he lost his job as a corporate auditor and started trying to use the tubes to do this full-time. Rob lives in a "small, small town" in the Bible Belt, and when people ask him what he does, he says he shoots wedding and special-event videos. ("If they only knew how Special. . . .")

On XTube, he puts up free previews meant to lure viewers to his pay-per-view content, which he sells for 50 cents a

---

Making Money as an XTube Amateur

- Viewer payment: $0.50 to $2.50 to view homemade content
- Monthly earnings for performers: $0 to upward of $2,000
- Revenue distribution: 50% to XTube, 50% to the performer (after XTube deducts a processing fee)
- XTube's overall monthly earnings for all types of content (professional and user-submitted): $140,000 to $160,000
- XTube's monthly earnings from homemade films: $56,000 to $64,000

(All numbers current as of January 2008)

TAKEN FROM: Compiled by editor.

---

minute. Rob says the average viewer watches ten minutes; of that $5, he gets to keep 50 percent, minus a small processing charge. A video he uploaded the week before we speak has been viewed 2,470 times, but a lot of the viewers watched only the free preview, so he has made just $125 from it. But he says he's earning around $1,500 every two weeks from XTube, more than he was making in his corporate gig. "The key is keeping new stuff up and answering your friend re-quests and private messages," he says. "It's good to know just how much they like my stuff, and what they would like to see in the future."

Homemade Porn as Career and Activism

If Rob is just getting started on XTube, a Boston male couple who go by the names Cole Maverick and Hunter are its Tila Tequilas. Cole, a former welder who got his masters in psychology, met Hunter, who had grown up in a devout Mormon family, when he was a college freshman. They've been together for ten years. Cole had always been a compulsive picture-taker, and four years ago, on a whim, he uploaded a few snapshots to XTube, followed by some movie clips and, later, movies featuring them with other men, often fans. They weren't prepared for the enormous popularity that has ensued. Their videos have been viewed more than 90 million times on XTube, where they are currently the "most favorited" submitter. "I remember the first time we posted one and got our first check. I said, 'Why doesn't everyone do this?'" Cole says. They now film full-time and clear "a nice six-figure income," according to Hunter.

"Our main goal," Cole says, "was to take gay sex out of the dark, leathery guilt-ridden realm, into fun sex, in the sun, in an honest, open relationship. We get so many inspiring messages from guys and girls who love what we're doing."

Paradoxically, as Cole and Hunter have thrived on the tubes, they have experienced the underbelly as well, increasingly finding their films pirated on tube sites, including XTube and PornHub. "They're big thieves," Cole says of the tubes. . . .

Online Pornography as Self-Expression

However the industry ultimately reshapes itself to accommodate the twin threats of free and stolen content, the broader legacy of the tubes may have little to do with the high-gloss, professionally made porn that they have imperiled. More than anything, the tubes have the potential to change the viewer's relationship to erotica itself. On some tubes, gigabytes of home movies are being uploaded and streamed without any money changing hands. There, consumers can also be producers. Posting can be as arousing as watching. We are all porn stars, if we want to be. Maybe porn isn't even really the right word for it anymore, as it evolves from something made to be watched to something made to be shared.

On XTube, of the videos submitted to the amateur portion of the site, only 20 percent are pay-per-view; the other 80 percent are evidently uploaded for kicks. Consider AlphaHarlot, a regular contributor to the site. Her real name is Liz. She's 30 and lives in Clifton, New Jersey, where by day she works as an accountant. Two years ago, she started uploading videos to XTube, which her boyfriend at the time had done. "When I joined I was in kind of a weird place," she says, "dating that guy plus a bunch of others that were more like one-night stands than relationships. And XTube gave me another outlet for that sexual energy, so I stopped slutting around in real life. XTube made me feel better about myself."

She eased into it, starting with photos. After loving the response she got, she moved to faceless videos, and ultimately to showing her face. She now has over 4,000 "friends" following her on XTube. She has been recognized twice in public, once in the Bath & Body Works at the Garden State Plaza. Some of the nearly 150 videos she has posted show her with a woman or with a man—she lives "a polyamorous lifestyle"—but most show her alone, masturbating or performing a fetish at the request of one of her fans.

Liz has never sought to make money from her videos. "I get excited making them, posting them, and seeing how people react," she says. She fears it would be less fun—more like a job—if she charged. "XTube is my family. It has completely altered how I see people. It's made me realize there are people out there who understand there's more to the world than black-and-white sexuality, that everyone fits in somewhere."

Still, even Liz, who lets people watch her videos for free, doesn't like to see her content show up on other websites. A few times a month, one of her vigilant XTube fans will alert her to an instance of piracy. Usually, after she contacts a site, they'll remove the video; sometimes they argue. "You want control of where your stuff appears," she says. "Stolen porn irks the hell out of me." She tries, at least once a month, to buy a DVD from an adult video store, "so I feel like I'm giving back a little."

Periodical and Internet Sources Bibliography

The following articles have been selected to supplement the diverse views presented in this chapter.

American Civil Liberties Union	"Teens Should Not Be Criminalized for Poor Judgment, Says ACLU," February 16, 2011. www.aclu.org.
Vaughan Bell	"Naomi Wolf, Porn and the Misuse of Dopamine," MindHacks.com, July 4, 2011. http://mindhacks.com.
Adi Bloom	"Risking Discovery: Why Would a Teacher Put Their Career in Jeopardy by Accessing Pornography in the Workplace?," *Times Educational Supplement* (UK), March 22, 2010.
Jacob Gershman	"Lawmakers Propose Teen 'Sexting' Law," *Wall Street Journal*, June 6, 2011.
Donald L. Hilton and Clark Watts	"Pornography Addiction: A Neuroscience Perspective," *Surgical Neurology International*, February 21, 2011.
Amanda Marcotte	"Lady Problems: If Larry Flynt, Hugh Hefner, and Bob Guccione Hadn't Had Personal Issues with Women, Would Today's Porn Be Less Awful?," *Slate*, November 16, 2011. www.slate.com.
Judith Reisman	"Erototoxin," Summer 2010. www.drjudithreisman.com.
Lisa Kirsch Satawa	"Sexting and Bullying: A Dangerous Combination—Teens: Trying to Be Cool Can Be Deadly," *Kirsch & Satawa Blog*, May 18, 2011. www.protectingyourfuture.info.
Naomi Wolf	"Is Pornography Driving Men Crazy?," *Global Public Square* (blog), June 30, 2011. http://globalpublicsquare.blogs.cnn.com.

OPPOSING
VIEWPOINTS®
SERIES

CHAPTER 3

Is Online Pornography a Special Threat to Minors?

Chapter Preface

It's an unspoken rule in American politics that an issue takes on considerable urgency when it is said to affect the safety and well-being of children. The debate about online pornography is no exception: Almost every argument—even those that are emphatically pro-pornography—is couched in terms of protecting children from exposure to sexually explicit material.

It's reasonable to want to protect children from all manner of injurious threats, from unmonitored band saws to tuberculosis. Where pornography is concerned, this desire presupposes two things: First, that pornography is somehow as inherently dangerous as a poorly secured power tool, and second, that adults—either directly or as a by-product—are highly likely to hurt otherwise innocent children. Numerous commentators have addressed whether or not pornography, in and of itself, is dangerous or harmful, but the question remains: Are children naive wanderers in need of protection from pornography, and by extension, protection from the adults who produce, peddle, and consume it?

At the mere suggestion that children do not need nearly the level of protection that some estimate, many commentators react with extreme concern, conjuring the image of an innocent preteen girl researching her science fair project, clicking the wrong link, and suddenly being assailed by a devastating image that causes permanent harm to her.

But is that what "minors being exposed to pornography" really means? According to the Internet Safety Technical Task Force's 2008 study "Enhancing Child Safety and Online Technologies," which was released by Harvard University's Berkman Center for Internet and Society:

> Review shows that the risks minors face online . . . are in most cases not significantly different than those they face

off-line, and that as they get older, minors themselves contribute to some of the problems. . . . The Internet increases the availability of harmful, problematic and illegal content, but does not always increase minors' exposure. Unwanted exposure to pornography does occur online, but those most likely to be exposed are those seeking it out, such as older male minors.

Furthermore, the study goes on to suggest that those minors who do uncover sexually explicit images are not passive victims of pornographic exposure but, perhaps of graver concern, active archivists and creators: "Most research focuses on adult pornography and violent content, but there are also concerns about other content, including child pornography and the violent, pornographic, and other problematic content that youth themselves generate," states the Internet safety task force.

While some authors featured in the following chapter strongly assert that pornography is dangerous and harmful to children, not all commentators are convinced that pornography itself poses any real risk to minors. Some even argue that access to pornography possibly serves to protect children from being victimized, pointing to studies that correlate a decrease in violent sex crimes against children with widespread access to pornography.

"It's easy for their perception of what is normal to get warped if they have no comparison other than what they've seen on the Internet."

Internet Pornography Warps Teen Sexuality

Sara Parker

Sara Parker produced the 2010 radio documentary Sex, Porn and Teenagers *for BBC Radio 4. The following viewpoint, written by Parker, is drawn from the* Times Educational Supplement *(or TES), a weekly British newspaper covering education and issues of interest to teachers. The author argues that the prevalence of online pornography has led many teens to use it as instructive material. She cites several experts who've seen the repercussions of this—ranging from minors being coerced and exploited to teens freely experimenting with sexual acts that they later find uncomfortable or unpleasant.*

As you read, consider the following questions:

1. According to Rebecca Avery, what is one reason that teenagers don't talk to adults about unsettling or threatening things they've seen online?

2. How many reports of online abuse does the Child Exploitation and Online Protection Centre see each year? How many cases requiring immediate action do they see each day?

3. Psychosexual therapist Dr. Frances Emeleus is concerned that repeated exposure to sexual imagery at a young age may lead to what?

When he was 11, Max used to sneak into his mother's bedroom when she was out and use her computer to Google words such as "cock and boobs". What he discovered was a world of web-based pornography, which he admits gave him unrealistic expectations of sex and relationships.

Unrealistic Expectations

"I was at that 'in-betweeny' stage between innocence and maturity," says Max, now 18. "Watching porn gave me a grand idea of what sex is. I thought, 'This is going to be brilliant', that I would be sitting there eating a pizza and some girl would come in and have sex with me.

"Obviously, that's completely unrealistic because the first time it's a bit stiff and rookie and very brief. But you've got to learn about sex from somewhere and for me it was from friends and the Internet."

It is hard to know how many teenagers regularly watch Internet porn, but the technology is moving so fast that many adults find it impossible to keep up with computer-savvy youngsters who can often get around parental controls and share pornography on their mobile phones.

Even hard-core and "special-interest" pornography is accessible. Damien, now 18, recalls how shocking it can be when seen for the first time. "Porn can spread around so easily. In Year 11, we sent videos around using our mobile phones and you'd look at it and wonder how anyone could do some of the things—the fact that young kids can get [their] hands on that footage is worrying."

Adding Online Pornography to Health Curriculum

Rebecca Avery, e-safety officer at Kent County Council, is concerned that youngsters are using pornography as a source of information and education. "It's easy for their perception of what is normal to get warped if they have no comparison other than what they've seen on the Internet or mates have loaded on to their mobile. We've got to teach them to be safe and discuss with them what they've seen."

She has found that even primary pupils have accessed pornography, sometimes by using the history on their parents' laptop or, as in the case of one nine-year-old, by working out the password to crack the parental controls on the home computer. At this age there can also be an element of bravado or cyber bullying.

"Sometimes they may get sent a link to something nasty or they'll be dared by a mate to type 'sex' into the search engine," she says. "If you type in anything to do with porn, it will come looking for you."

As one of the first local authority e-safety officers in the UK [United Kingdom], Ms Avery runs training courses for teachers and others working in schools, as well as providing education for parents and pupils.

She would like the issues of porn and social networking sites to be built into sex and relationships education as a matter of course, but she says some teachers are wary of such discussions, preferring to wait until individual pupils raise them.

Parents in Denial

She also finds that parents are often in denial, refusing to accept that their teenage child is accessing pornography or using their mobile phone to share sexually explicit images.

"No one likes to think of their child watching pornography," she says. "The biggest problem with the Internet is that children and teenagers don't feel they can tell anyone if they see something they shouldn't. Their assumption is the computer or mobile will be taken away from them. Parents often feel their children are safer on the computer because they're at home—that may not be the case."

That it may not be the case has prompted many schools in Kent to take up the e-safety training and support on offer, while pupils are encouraged to report anything online that makes them feel threatened or uncomfortable.

At one primary, this open-door policy led a 10-year-old girl to report an online friendship which immediately rang alarm bells with head Richard Sutton Smith. "They were asking to meet her," he says. "It may have been innocent but we informed the police and told the girl to reply saying she wanted nothing more to do with the contact, who started sending e-mails with explicit content.

"Unfortunately, there were 11 or so other girls in the online friendship group who were also flooded with something like 20 links to explicit sites," he says.

Mr Sutton Smith copied all the parents into the exchanges. "I knew that none of them would be aware that their child was gaining access to that sort of stuff simply by trying to have friends," he adds.

Subterfuge in Social Networks

When it comes to the Pandora's box of Internet porn, Ms Avery finds that older boys are more likely to push the boundaries, while girls tend to sign up on social networking sites. Age restrictions seem to pose few barriers. Parents may give in to the pressure of the "all my friends are doing it" argument and sign up their children to sites such as Facebook even though they are under age—Facebook has a lower-age limit of 13. She even came across a four-year-old on Facebook, signed up by his 10-year-old brother, who in turn had been registered by his parents.

Many free pornography websites only require children and teenagers to tick a box to say they are over 18. Even where they have to complete a form to register, they can lie.

"We must make them realise that if they can lie, so can the other people they meet online," says Ms Avery.

And much of this is hidden from both teachers and parents. "There's loads of things adults don't know about," says Jemima, 14. "I've had friends who've met up with older guys they've met online and someone was asked to send pictures of herself topless—she didn't because she didn't want to embarrass herself, but she carried on talking to him."

Internet Pornography Leads to Exploitation

Another teenager tells how a 15-year-old girl in her school was videoed by her boyfriend having sex and the footage was Bluetoothed around his whole year. "She put a brave face on it although she was obviously very distressed. I don't think her parents or teachers knew," she says.

These are the kind of stories Vicky Gillings, of the Child Exploitation and Online Protection Centre (CEOP), hears daily. As a policing authority funded by the government, it receives more than 6,000 reports of online abuse a year, some directly from children, others from parents, teachers or other professionals.

Every day, the centre has at least four cases on which it must take immediate action because a child is at such severe risk, either from a possible sex offender or because the situation has become so bad that they are threatening suicide.

"Children and teenagers are vulnerable online," Ms Gillings says. "They often don't realise the risks of sharing sexually provocative images that can do the rounds, be manipulated and end up on a paedophile website.

"They are open to blackmail and coercion. They may be told that if they don't do something, their account will be deleted or their profile page hacked into. The screen and key-

"You don't need to tell me about the birds and the bees. I downloaded it all from the internet," cartoon by Aaron Bacall. www.cartoonstockcom. Copyright © Aaron Bacall. Reproduction rights obtainable from www.CartoonStock.com.

board give an illusion of safety and anonymity, but there are hugely powerful grooming techniques that can sexualise or normalise what this child is being asked to do."

The Pressure to Appear Sexually Savvy

In Kent, it was an incident in which girls were asked to pose online for sexually explicit images that prompted the local authority to appoint an e-safety officer. The girls were targeted by a 21-year-old man in Canada, who has since been convicted and sentenced to three years' imprisonment for extortion, blackmail and creating indecent images.

Ms Gillings believes there is huge pressure on young people to appear sexually available, not only from their peer group but from an increasingly sexualised celebrity culture. She says: "It only takes a celebrity to say they go on a site such as Chatroulette for youngsters to go on that site in the hope of meeting that celebrity."

Ms Avery has come across youngsters organising Chatroulette parties. Intended to be a harmless random communication using webcam, the site was soon taken up by people masturbating or performing other sexual acts in front of the camera. She says that when youngsters stumble across such images, it is difficult for them not to watch, even though it is real people doing real things in their front room.

"It's what I call the 'car crash effect'," she says. "'I can't believe what I am watching'—so they keep on watching."

Exploring Sexuality Through Internet Pornography

A lot of pornography holds similar fascination for sexually curious teenagers, even when it is accidentally accessed or unsolicited. One 14-year-old girl kept on being sent pop-ups and links to porn sites by another pupil during their MSN conversations. "It was horrible and you can't get rid of those images," says the girl, now 18.

While the assumption is that it is mainly boys who are consumers of pornography, girls are by no means aloof from it all, even if they see it as "a bit of a giggle", something to add spice to a sleepover.

"I remember when I first saw porn at one of my friend's sleepovers and we were just looking it up for a joke," says one 17-year-old girl. "There was about 20 of us and literally you can just type in anything and see all kinds of porn. We were just messing around, but if you watch it when boys are about they often try to lad it up and it's just embarrassing."

She went on to watch more pornography with her gay best friend. "We were lying on his bed when he asked me if I wanted to watch gay porn—and I said yes," she says. "I find it quite interesting, the different categories. Some can be sexy but some are ridiculous. I've been shocked by sadist pornography and I did see some men cut their girlfriends, but the more you watch it the less shocking it becomes—the human brain can only maintain the shock factor for a couple of seconds."

Desensitisation Poses Risks

Psychosexual therapist Dr Frances Emeleus, who has worked with youngsters addicted to pornography, is concerned that such desensitisation can normalise extreme sexual behaviour as well as leading to unrealistic expectations of themselves and their partner.

She is concerned that repeated exposure to sex at a young age can lead to "a split between feeling and excitement".

"When there is no feeling, the pornographic image has to escalate to fill the whole sexual field and produce the same hit of excitement," she says. "The danger of repeated exposure to pornography for young people is that they will see the other person as an exciting object to be discarded once they cease to be exciting. And when it comes to choosing a partner, you have a shopping list of what they should be like, what they should do or not do."

Broadening Horizon for Better and Worse

But one 18-year-old, who is now in a steady relationship, believes his exposure to pornography has improved his sex life. "You want to experiment with things—different positions, different types of oral sex," he says. "When you see bondage and that sort of stuff, you think 'I'd never do it' because it looks like it's hurting, but when you're having sex you may try different things like pulling your partner's hair to see if it does turn you on, if it spices things up or not."

Dr Emeleus is concerned that some girls are now being asked to do things during sex with which they are uncomfortable. "Sexual experimentation between young people has been going on forever, but there's something about the extreme images which is disturbing," she says. "Learning about them is one thing, but ramping it up to avoid dealing with the issues of relationships and needing the buzz of that excitement is not a safe way to go."

The proliferation of Internet pornography may also be behind the rise in the number of girls as young as 13 coming to health professionals having had anal sex as a way of avoiding getting pregnant.

Simon Blake, chief executive of sexual health charity Brook, says anal sex is seen as less intimate than oral sex. "It's a cultural problem that we don't talk to young people about sex in ways in which they can protect themselves early on," he says.

Embedding Feelings of Inadequacy

He believes pornography can create feelings of inadequacy around body image. Brook has also seen girls who are worried about having pubic hair after seeing waxed porn actresses. For boys, the feelings of inadequacy often revolve around penis size.

Mr Blake would like to see more age-appropriate sex and relationships education from primary school onwards. "We've got to start talking about the way the body works from early on so we can discuss the gritty issues later," he says.

"We've got to help young people understand that pornography isn't real life. It is a horrible way of boys learning about sex which objectifies women a lot of the time—and can be very frightening."

"The sexual dangers to youth, online or off, may be less than we think. Yet adults routinely conflate friendly sex play with hurtful online behavior."

The Threat of Online Sexual Content Is Exaggerated

Judith Levine

Judith Levine is a writer and civil libertarian. She is the author of several books, including Harmful to Minors: The Perils of Protecting Children from Sex. *In the following viewpoint, Levine argues that despite conventional wisdom insisting that teen exposure to online pornography inexorably leads to exploitation, victimization, and misery, there is little evidence to support this. She points to a variety of scientific studies that have found American teens are less sexually active than in previous generations.*

As you read, consider the following questions:

1. What does a report issued by Harvard University's Berkman Center for Internet and Society have to say about teens who have sex with adults they meet online? Did the study find that minors frequently stumbled across pornography accidentally?

2. According to the Centers for Disease Control and Prevention, how much more likely is a child from a family with an annual income less than $15,000 to be sexually abused, compared to a child whose family earns more than $30,000?

3. Has La Salle University sociologist and criminal justice professor Kathleen A. Bogle found that today's teens are more or less conservative than their parents were at their age?

A couple of weeks ago, [in early 2009] in Greensburg, Pennsylvania, prosecutors charged six teenagers with creating, distributing, and possessing child pornography. The three girls, ages 14 and 15, took nude or seminude pictures of themselves and e-mailed them to friends, including three boys, ages 16 and 17, who are among the defendants. Police Captain George Seranko described the obscenity of the images: They "weren't just breasts," he declared. "They showed female anatomy!"

Bullying Is a Bigger Threat than Pedophiles

Greensburg's crime-stoppers aren't the only ones looking out for the cybersafety of America's youth. In Alabama, Connecticut, Florida, New Jersey, New York, Michigan, Ohio, Pennsylvania, Texas, and Utah (at last count) minors have been arrested for "sexting," or sending or posting soft-core photo or video self-portraits. Of 1,280 teens and young adults surveyed recently by the National Campaign to Prevent Teen and Unplanned Pregnancy, one in five said they engaged in the practice—girls only slightly more than boys.

Seranko and other authorities argue that such pictures may find their way to the Internet and from there to pedophiles and other exploiters. "It's very dangerous," he opined.

How dangerous is it? Not very, suggests a major study released this month [February 2009] by Harvard's Berkman

Center for Internet [and Society]. "Enhancing Child Safety and Online Technologies," the result of a yearlong investigation by a wide range of experts, concludes that "the risks minors face online are in most cases not significantly different from those they face off-line, and as they get older, minors themselves contribute to some of the problems." Almost all youth who end up having sex with adults they meet online seek such assignations themselves, fully aware that the partner is older. Similarly, minors who encounter pornography online go looking for it; they tend to be older teenage boys.

But sex and predatory adults are not the biggest dangers kids face as they travel the Net. Garden-variety kid-on-kid meanness, enhanced by technology, is. "Bullying and harassment, most often by peers, are the most frequent threats that minors face, both online and off-line," the report found.

Risky Online Behavior Is the Result, Not the Cause, of Other Social Problems

Just as almost all physical and sexual abuse is perpetrated by someone a child knows intimately—the adult who eats dinner or goes to church with her—victims of cyberbullying usually know their tormenters: other students who might sit beside them in homeroom or chemistry. Social networking sites may be the places where kids are likely to hurt each other these days, but those sites, like the bullying, "reinforce pre-existing social relations," according to the report.

Similarly, young people who get in sexual or social trouble online tend to be those who are already at risk off-line—doing poorly in school, neglected or abused at home, and/or economically impoverished. According to the Centers for Disease Control and Prevention, a child from a family whose annual income is less than $15,000 is 22 times more likely to suffer sexual abuse than a child whose parents earn more than $30,000.

Other new research implies that online sexual communication, no matter how much there is, isn't translating into corporeal sex, with either adults or peers. Contrary to popular media depiction of girls and boys going wilder and wilder, La Salle University sociologist and criminal justice professor Kathleen A. Bogle has found that American teens are more conservative than their elders were at their age. Teen virginity is up and the number of sexual partners is down, she discovered. Only the rate of births to teenage girls has risen in the last few years—a result of declining contraceptive use. This may have something to do with abstinence-only education, which leaves kids reluctant or incompetent when it comes to birth control. Still, the rate of teen births compared to pregnancies always tracks the rate among adult women, and it's doing that now, too.

Like the kids finding adult sex partners in chat rooms, those who fail to protect themselves from pregnancy or sexually transmitted diseases and have their babies young tend to be otherwise at risk emotionally or socially. In other words, kids who are having a rough time in life are having a rough time in virtual life as well. Sexual or emotional harm *precedes* risky or harmful online and off-line behavior, rather than the other way around.

Harsh Sex Crime Laws Can Devastate Teens' Lives

Enter the law—and the injuries of otherwise harmless teenage sexual shenanigans begin. The effects of the ever-stricter sex crimes laws, which punish ever-younger offenders, are tragic for juveniles. A child pornography conviction—which could come from sending a racy photo of yourself or receiving said photo from a girlfriend or boyfriend—carries far heavier penalties than most hands-on sexual offenses. Even if a juvenile sees no lock-up time, he or she will be forced to register as a sex offender for 10 years or more. The federal Adam

Walsh Child Protection [and Safety] Act of 2007 requires that sex offenders as young as 14 register.

As documented in such reports as Human Rights Watch's "No Easy Answers: Sex Offender Laws in the United States" and "Registering Harm: How Sex Offense Registries Fail Youth and Communities" from the Justice Policy Institute, conviction and punishment for a sex crime (a term that includes nonviolent offenses such as consensual teen sex, flashing, and patronizing a prostitute) effectively squashes a minor's chances of getting a college scholarship, serving in the military, securing a good job, finding decent housing, and, in many cases, moving forward with hope or happiness.

Despite Study Findings, Many Adults Panic About Teen Sexuality

The sexual dangers to youth, online or off, may be less than we think. Yet adults routinely conflate friendly sex play with hurtful online behavior. "Teaching Teenagers About Harassment," a recent piece in the *New York Times*, swings between descriptions of consensual photo-swapping and incessant, aggressive texting and Facebook or MySpace rumor- and insult-mongering as if these were similarly motivated—and equally harmful. It quotes the San Francisco–based Family Violence Prevention Fund [currently known as Futures Without Violence], which calls sending nude photos "whether it is done under pressure or not" an element of "digital dating violence."

Sober scientific data do nothing to calm such anxieties. Reams of comments flowed into the *New York Times* when it reported Dr. Bogle's findings. "The way TV and MUSIC is promoting sex and explicit content daily and almost on every network," read one typical post, from the aptly named MsKnowledge, "I would have to say this article is completely naive. The streets are talking and there [sic] saying teens and young adults are becoming far more involved in more adult and sexual activities than most ADULTS. Scientific data is a JOKE . . . pay attention to reality and the REAL world will tell you otherwise."

A better-educated interlocutor, NPR's *On the Media* host Brooke Gladstone, defaulted to the same assumption in an interview with one of the Harvard Internet task force members, Family Online Safety Institute CEO Stephen Balkam. What lessons could be drawn from the study's findings? Gladstone asked. "What can be and what should be done to protect kids?"

"There's no silver bullet that's going to solve this issue," Balkam replied. But "far more cooperation has got to happen between law enforcement, industry, the academic community, and we need to understand far better the psychological issues that are at play here."

It's unclear from this exchange what Gladstone believes kids need to be protected from or what issue Balkam is solving. But neither of them came to the logical conclusion of the Harvard study: that we should back off, moderate our fears, and stop thinking of youthful sexual expression as a criminal matter. Still, Balkam wants to call in the cops.

Maybe all that bullying is a mirror of the way adults treat young people minding their own sexual business. Maybe the "issue" is not sex but adults' response to it: the harm we do trying to protect teenagers from themselves.

> *"Today, it is not unheard of for boys to become hooked on autoerotic asphyxiation, bondage, or rape porn."*

Online Porn Is Toxic to Kids

Marnia Robinson

Marnia Robinson is the author of Cupid's Poisoned Arrow: From Habit to Harmony in Sexual Relationships. *In the following viewpoint, first published by the* Good Men Project, *an online magazine dedicated to exploring what it means to be a "good man," Robinson explains that online pornography poses a real threat to the development of today's boys. While one might be tempted to dismiss online pornography as substantially no different from erotic literature of years past or men's magazines like* Playboy, *Robinson argues that this new, ever-accessible, and often extreme pornography is fundamentally different.*

As you read, consider the following questions:

1. What does Robinson say about the availability of scientific research to support the notion that pornography harms kids?

Marnia Robinson, "Boys and Porn: It Ain't Your Father's 'Playboy,'" GoodMenProject .com, December 3, 2010. Copyright © 2010 by the Good Men Project. All rights reserved. Reproduced by permission.

2. According to sexologist Jakob Pastötter, how has pornography shaped and altered mainstream sexual perceptions and practices in the last sixty years?

3. What are two major differences between modern online porn and the pornography of the past, such as *Playboy* magazine?

About five years ago [in 2005], limitless quantities of free, shocking, explicit videos became widely available to savvy Internet users with high-speed connections. Alas, some of the planet's most talented computer wizards are youngsters (or their buddies). Passing around outrageous pornographic video clips is now a popular social activity.

Extreme Stimulation

Such videos are often so extreme that they dumbfound even the most freethinking parents. According to psychiatrist Norman Doidge in *The Brain That Changes Itself*, porn grows more shocking because today's porn users tend to habituate to material viewed. That is, today's super-stimulating porn, instead of satisfying more, numbs the brain's pleasure response. Then the user needs something even more shocking to get aroused—which the porn industry readily delivers. Who's gonna get excited by *Pac-Man* when he has been playing *Grand Theft Auto* or *Halo 3*?

Increasingly, extreme porn is a problem. The more novel, startling, forbidden, or disgusting a video is, the cooler it is to pass around, and the more it excites a viewer's brain (specifically, the reward circuitry). Climax then reinforces the "value" of the material that produces the climax. So, kids' brains are now rewiring to value brain-jolting material, for which nothing in their (or most anyone's) experience has prepared them. The constant flood of novel material keeps dopamine levels in the reward circuitry high while viewing continues, reinforcing the lesson that these images are valuable and important. Norepinephrine released in response to shocking images also appears to reinforce this learning.

Erectile Dysfunction and Social Anxiety in Younger Teens

While video games also flood the brain with dopamine, it's evident that sexual content activates additional aspects of the brain's reward circuitry. As kids mature, sexual reproduction signals trump video game thrills.

The brain changes that follow repeated stimulation can have surprising effects. Young men report that their sexual tastes sometimes morph in unexpected directions, and that they become less responsive to normal flirting.

Since I began sharing the correlations men are discovering between heavy Internet porn use and symptoms like erectile dysfunction [ED] and social anxiety, I've been hearing from younger and younger guys struggling with such symptoms. (As an aside, users who manage to avoid extreme stimulation do not seem to report unusual erectile dysfunction problems.) Here's a sample:

> I'm hoping to recover and get aroused more around girls. I have been going insane thinking that my sex life is over. I am 15 years old and I've been masturbating since I was 12. It started out as just simple videos but now I have been getting into more extreme stuff. . . . Can you explain to me the basic steps I need to take to recover please?. . . I have to ask this so that my mind can rest and I can feel confident. Is there any permanent damage done to me? If I successfully quit porn will my limb stay up when I become sexually active in the future? Or will I have ED issues?

Science has not investigated or verified the answers to his questions. First, who can find porn virgins of a suitable age to test? Second, who deliberately wants to expose kids to hyper-stimulating, abnormal, erotic videos to see what happens in

A Link Between Porn and the Torture Committed by American Soldiers at Abu Ghraib

Imagine for a moment a guard's night of pornographic entertainment at Abu Ghraib [a detention facility in Baghdad, Iraq]. The [American] soldier sits down at his computer, onto which is loaded a variety of the photographs and videos that became familiar to us once the scandal was exposed. The first button he (or she) touches on the computer will automatically remove from the screen abuse photos used as screensavers. (The heap of naked Iraqis was apparently a favorite.) Now, if he wants to be titillated, he can view some pornography. He could go to the Internet, the source of the vast majority of violent pornography today, or he might simply call up the amateur porn files created by the guards themselves, featuring one another as "actors." . . . In either case, the porn files exist side by side with abuse files, setting up an easy-to-imagine evening of entertainment: a little porn, a little abuse, a little more porn, a little torture, and then some more porn. Given the pleasure taken by the guards in both their homemade porn images and those of detainee abuse, such evenings, depressing as it is to contemplate, almost certainly were routine. . . .

At Abu Ghraib, the interspersion of traditional heterosexual porn, often featuring the guards themselves, with sexual degradation and violence against Iraqi detainees can be said to reflect that segment of the professional porn world that mixes sex with (usually) simulated violence.

Carmine Sarracino and Kevin M. Scott,
The Porning of America: The Rise of Porn Culture,
What It Means, and Where We Go from Here.
Boston: Beacon Press, 2008.

their brains, or how it alters their sexual response? No one is measuring the ways in which extreme videos may subtly be changing brain sensitivity, thereby altering libido and sexual tastes over time.

Porn Shapes Perception

Again, it's likely that the missing insights revolve around an ancient mechanism found in all mammalian brains: the reward circuit. It has long been known that overstimulating it with drugs can cause increased cravings. Now, research is revealing that non-drug, "natural" things, like junk food, can alter this part of the brain like drugs—numbing the response to normal stimuli.

If a guy has been viewing porn videos since puberty, how would he know if his (lack of) response to potential sweethearts, his kinky tastes, or his masturbation cravings are normal for him? He has nothing with which to compare. Sexologist Jakob Pastötter gives an example of how porn shapes perception:

> When Kinsey did his studies in the '40s, not even gay men practiced anal sex frequently. The first changes occurred during the '70s in the gay scene and then, especially under the influence of the so-called gonzo pornography, also in heterosexual circles. Suddenly, anal sex seems to have become quite a common practice. And accordingly, sex counselors report that not too long ago the first boys inquired, "How can I persuade my girlfriend to have anal sex?" Then, a few years later, came the first girls: "How can I dissuade my boyfriend from anal sex?" Now, the girls come and ask the sex counselors, "What pills can I take to prevent it hurting like hell?" All this in a period of only fifteen years, which began when anal sex was introduced in pornography as a common sex variant, in the mid-'90s approximately.

Today, it is not unheard of for boys to become hooked on autoerotic asphyxiation, bondage, or rape porn. Psychologists have published accounts of otherwise straight boys who developed unsettling obsessions when desensitized to vanilla imagery—and then felt such intense, pervasive anxiety that their real-life relationships were compromised.

Healthy and Unhealthy Masturbation

Most parents cross their fingers, remind themselves that they survived encounters with *Playboy*, and hope their kids will figure things out for themselves.

But today's porn is nothing like *Playboy*. It's video, so the viewer can more easily imagine himself in a role—especially in modern, envelope-pushing "gonzo"-style films, where the actors hold the cameras. It's always novel, and there's no limit to how much can be viewed. In other words, *not all masturbation is equal.*

Masturbation based on imagining affectionate contact with a real potential mate is stimulating enough, especially for a teenager. But masturbation based on shocking stimuli, by gradually numbing the brain, can shift the user's priorities away from real potential mates.

Should caregivers shame kids or imply they are bad people for watching today's porn? Certainly not. But caregivers should tell kids to avoid Internet porn as much as possible, and why. Even if science is lagging behind in reliable research, anecdotal evidence of Internet porn's risks is increasing. It's also becoming clear that there are unmistakable benefits from leaving it behind.

Directing Kids Toward Healthy Sexuality

1. *Find a balance.* Tell kids that masturbation is normal, and that it's beneficial to work out a schedule that doesn't escalate. Tell them to experiment with different intervals of say, once or twice a week, or even less. Point out that sometimes less frequent masturbation actually results in less overall frustration. Sticking with a sched-

ule will require some self-discipline, a skill kids will use throughout life. Consider teaching your child one of the many ancient techniques for redistributing sexual energy.

2. *Understand the escalation problem.* Point out that our brains are generally calibrated for genitals achieving normal degrees of stimulation and arousal. Once we move to new thresholds of stimulation (today's super-porn or sex toys), we risk making our brains temporarily less sensitive to subtler, ordinary stimuli.

3. *Stick to natural stimuli.* Tell kids to masturbate based on their own imaginings of real potential mates and realistic, affectionate sexual encounters. If that isn't getting them to climax, it's probably because their brains haven't returned to full sensitivity since their previous climax. Nonetheless, it is better to wait than to turn to today's porn to get the job done.

4. *Porn is unrealistic.* Point out that a partner's satisfaction is not dependent upon the huge, unflagging erection or other characteristics of a porn star. Nor is a man's pleasure dependent upon the hairless genitals, breast implants, or degradation of his partner. Paint a mental picture of normal sex for your child.

5. *Masturbation is not the ideal mood medicine.* Because climax offers temporary relief, it seems like a cure for anxiety. Kids can easily get in the habit of masturbating to regulate mood. Unfortunately, too frequent climax can make tension worse over the following days. Kids need other ways to regulate mood. Vigorous exercise, friendly interaction with others, trusted companionship, time in nature, affectionate touch/hugs, doing something creative, singing, time with pets, meditation, and service

to others have all been shown to help reduce stress and/or regulate mood—probably because they improve brain balance.

6. *Avoid threats and shaming.* Risky activities release extra adrenaline and dopamine into the brain, and are therefore paradoxically perceived as more "valuable." (The brain's primitive reward circuitry assesses value based upon how much dopamine is released in connection with an activity.) Threats of future punishment and warnings against "sin" therefore increase porn's power to overstimulate the brain, making subsequent porn binging more likely. . . .

Research shows that a strong, supportive parental relationship can protect kids against risky behavior, even in those who are genetically vulnerable. So, whether or not you find the above suggestions helpful, do find a way to discuss today's gonzo-porn videos with your child without shaming or threatening. Encourage your child to ask questions. Accept that ultimately he will have to make his own decisions. All you can do is offer solid information, your loving support, and a healthy example. That may be all your child needs to steer toward sexual balance.

"Certainly [it] is correct that more extreme forms of pornography are more easily available than ever before. But are we so sure that's a bad thing?"

Online Porn Is Not Toxic, Even to Kids

Christopher Shulgan

Christopher Shulgan is a writer and the parenting columnist for Toronto's the Grid. *He has written and ghostwritten many books, including* Superdad: A Memoir of Rebellion, Drugs and Fatherhood. *In the following viewpoint, Shulgan directly addresses Marnia Robinson's claims that there is a fundamental difference between modern online pornography and the pornography of the past. He concludes that this hysteria—which lacks a solid factual basis—is rooted in the perpetual and unfounded claim that "things were different when I was a kid."*

As you read, consider the following questions:

1. What is one *advantage* the author cites to the amount and variety of pornography available online?

2. What is the author's counterexample to Marnia Robinson's claim that Internet porn "burns out" natural erotic response?

3. What does the author believe history shows about Robinson's argument?

This is a response to [an] article by Marnia Robinson on the *Good Men Project* magazine, entitled, "Boys and Porn: It Ain't Your Father's 'Playboy.'" To sum up, Ms. Robinson's argument basically is this: Today's pornography is more extreme than what existed a generation ago, and that's bad for our adolescent males, because it could lead to decreased sensitivity to erotic stimuli and other forms of sexual dysfunction.

Broadly, my responses to Ms. Robinson's article fall into three categories.

Is Internet Porn So Bad?

Certainly Ms. Robinson is correct that more extreme forms of pornography are more easily available than ever before. But are we so sure that's a bad thing? In fact, perhaps it's kind of awesome. All over the wired world, young men and women are entering a culture where easily available imagery depicts every kind of sexual fetish imaginable. Some of it is hilarious, some of it is a little alarming, some of it is just plain strange. And dangerous—certainly, autoerotic asphyxiation qualifies as that. But before we demonize all this variety, can we also acknowledge there are advantages to it as well? Our easier-than-ever ability to access all kinds of crazy pornography also removes much of the loneliness and stigma of strangeness. Teenagers troubled by an erotic response to whatever are now able to hop online, type a few keywords into Google and discover a community out there of like-minded people, which they can then explore in a healthy, stigma-free fashion. So yes, this easy access to pornographic variety can be dangerous in extreme cases—but it can also help kids develop their sexualities in ways that are more healthy than before.

Accidental Artistic Merit of Pornography

Mr. Harold Hecuba, whose magazine job entails reviewing dozens of adult releases every month, has an interesting vignette about a Los Angeles Police Dept. [LAPD] detective he met once when H.H.'s car got broken into and a whole box of Elegant Angel Inc. videotapes was stolen ... and subsequently recovered by the LAPD. A detective brought the box back to Hecuba personally ... the detective had really just used the box's return as an excuse to meet Hecuba, whose critical work he appeared to know, and to discuss the ins and outs of the adult-video industry. It turned out that this detective—60, happily married, a grandpa, shy, polite, clearly a decent guy— was a hard-core fan. He and Hecuba ended up over coffee, and when H.H. finally cleared his throat and asked the cop why such an obviously decent fellow squarely on the side of law and civic virtue was a porn fan, the detective confessed that what drew him to the films was "the faces," i.e., the actresses' faces, i.e., those rare moments in orgasm or accidental tenderness when the starlets dropped their stylized ... sneer and became, suddenly, real people. "Sometimes—and you never know when, is the thing—sometimes all of a sudden they'll kind of reveal themselves" was the detective's way of putting it. "Their what-do-you-call ... humanness." It turned out that the LAPD detective found adult films *moving*, in fact far more so than most mainstream Hollywood movies. ... "In real movies, it's all on purpose. I suppose what I like in porno is the accident of it."

David Foster Wallace,
Consider the Lobster and Other Essays.
New York: Little, Brown & Co., 2005.

Does Internet Porn Really Burn You Out?

Ms. Robinson attempts to use science to establish that pornography is able to "burn out" our responses to other erotic stimuli. But the scientific evidence she uses is so sketchy even she acknowledges the problems with it: "[S]cience is lagging behind in reliable research," she writes, then says: "anecdotal evidence of Internet porn's risks is increasing." In my experience, yes, an element of novelty is required to trigger an erotic response. But this novelty-reward cycle exists in many other areas of our lives. Design, for example. The novelty in the stark modernism of a [Ludwig] Mies van der Rohe–designed building like Toronto's T-D [Toronto-Dominion] Centre or New York's Seagram Building, can trigger in me a response of sublime admiration. But that doesn't lead me on an addictive quest for ever more extreme examples of stark modernism.

In fact, it may even direct my quest for novelty in the opposite direction—toward the far more ornate Louis XIV–era Palace of Versailles, perhaps. In the same way, the novelty that triggers an erotic response from some really hard-core S&M [sadomasochism] might later lead someone toward the comparatively more vanilla eroticism of, say, strawberry eating.

History Proves Ms. Robinson Wrong

Broadly, Ms. Robinson's reasoning follows the template of an argument that history has proven erroneous, generation after generation. Basically, the outlines of her argument are this: *Yes, we had X, and we turned out fine. But the kind of X that exists now is different, and that difference is really going to mess up our children!* Parents for generations have been recalling the stuff *they* did as kids, and then undergoing some truly gymnastic reasoning, to determine a way *their kids'* stuff is really going to f--- them up. (Similar lines of reasoning have been employed when discussing marijuana, or violent video games.) Often the point of this argument is: LET'S BAN IT! Ms. Robinson manages to be relatively temperate in her response. Kudos to her for that. But come on. Sure, today we have easier access to a wider variety of pornography than ever before. As the headline suggests, today's *Naughty America* is not your father's *Playboy*. But then again, your father's *Playboy* wasn't *his* father's titillating postcard. When *Playboy* came along, the '60s equivalent of Ms. Robinson were all up in arms about how terrible it was that young men could get erotic magazines at newsstands. And hey, those men turned out all right. And you know what? Our kids today will turn out OK, too.

> *"The rates of rape, sexual assault, and other sex crimes either decreased or essentially remained stable following the ready availability of erotic materials of all sorts."*

The Availability of Child Pornography Lowers the Incidence of Sex Crimes Against Children

Milton Diamond, Eva Jozifkova, and Petr Weiss

Milton Diamond is well known for his extensive writing—academic, legal, and general interest—on family planning, pornography, intersexuality, and transsexuality. In the following viewpoint, Diamond and his coauthors, Eva Jozifkova and Petr Weiss, explore the apparent relationship between pornography and sexual violence. Noting that many studies have found a correlation between increased access to pornography and decreased incidence of sexual violence, the authors look at the specific case of the Czech Republic from 1971–2007. During this period,

Czechs saw almost unfettered access to pornography including child pornography, yet Diamond and his team found a marked decrease in all sex crimes, especially sexual violence against children.

As you read, consider the following questions:

1. What are some of the several countries cited by the authors decreases in sexual violence?

2. How did the authors establish that pornography was more readily available in the Czech Republic following the fall of communism?

3. According to the findings of a 2009 Swiss study, does viewing child pornography appear to be a risk factor in the sexual abuse of a child?

One of the most contentious areas of expression and free speech is that related to the presentation of sexual matters. Different factions in many societies object in different ways. Some are opposed to any graphic or open depiction or discussion of topics remotely related to sex; others desire an end to even, minor restrictions on such displays. Certainly, people differ widely on what might be considered pornographic; some people even see popular magazines like *Playboy* [as] pornographic. Extremists in the debate argue that pornography is a catalyst promoting sex crimes and rape in particular. Such persons have their own broad definition of pornography. . . .

Researching Pornography's Impact

In an effort to study this issue, research has often been to expose subjects—usually university students—to SEM [sexually explicit material] and then, with pencil and paper survey testing, evaluate their responses to questions posed as if these would be a reflection of their actual behavior. A more fruitful method, started by the Danish researcher [B.] Kutchinsky, was to see what actually happened in those countries that transitioned from having a strict ban on SEM availability to a situation where the material was decriminalized. Using data gathered from various governmental records, Kutchinsky compared the relevant increase in available SEM following the liberalization of antipornography laws in Denmark, Sweden, West Germany, and the U.S. with both pre- and post-liberalization data regarding sex crimes reported in these countries. His research found that, in the countries studied, the rates of rape, sexual assault, and other sex crimes either decreased or essentially remained stable following the ready availability of erotic materials of all sorts. In none did sex crimes of any type increase.

Other countries have been investigated to see if Kutchinsky's findings would hold across diverse cultures and traditions. Three Asian locations studied, Japan; Shanghai, China; and Hong Kong with very different histories and social structures from those studied earlier, [research] also found that available government records showed that while the amount and availability of pornography increased, the rates of sexual crimes decreased. Reassessment of the situation in the U.S. also supported this pattern, as did studies conducted in Croatia and Finland.

The current article reports findings from a Slavic country, the Czech Republic, with its own religious and cultural traditions unlike any previously studied. During the 1948–1989 Communist regime, the laws and customs were extremely puritanical. Pornography by any definition was absolutely prohibited. Even the depiction of naked bodies, as well as descriptions of sexual activities in fictional novels or magazines, were almost nonexistent. With the 1989 transition to democracy in the country the ban on pornography was lifted and a sexual permissiveness followed. In 1990, the availability and ownership of SEM increased explosively. Even the possession of child pornography was not a criminal offense.

Twentieth-Century Czechoslovakia

Czechoslovakia (*Ceskoslovensko*) had been a sovereign federated government formed in 1918 and consisting of two separate states. On 1 January 1993, the federation peacefully split into the Czech Republic and Slovakia. Prior to the division, all judicial and police data were kept separate for each state and compiled for national statistics. For the present study, only the pre- and post-separation population and crime data pertinent to the Czech Republic were used.

The time ranges used for this investigation basically started in the mid-1970s, a 15-year period in which various sex-related materials, even items like *Playboy* magazine, were banned. With the end of communism and the coming of democracy in November and December 1989, application of the laws regarding the dissemination and availability of pornography were considerably loosened so that even the possession of child pornography was not illegal. This period covers 18 years of major sociopolitical changes, including the country's Velvet Revolution, first free elections, establishment of a democratic government to replace communism (1990), and peaceful separation from Slovakia. Our study period ended with data from 2007. [In 2007 the Czech Republic passed a law prohibiting the possession of child pornography.]

Czech Law in the Last Half of the Twentieth Century

In the Czech Republic, the laws concerning pornography are somewhat vague. The Czech Criminal Code (Act No. 140/1961, as amended) leaves the exact definition of these legal terms to case law and to jurisprudence. As a result, it does not explicitly define pornographic works. According to Czech legal practice, a pornographic work can be any product that directly or by means of technical devices (e.g., film, video, the Internet) affects and stimulates the sexual instinct in a very intense and obtrusive manner. Essentially, any "material endangering morality" may be considered excessively sexually graphic and subject to criminal penalty. Section 205 of the Czech Criminal Code is the principal regulation applicable to the distribution of pornography. The basis for this law has been in existence since 1961. In practice, the law essentially prohibits the production, dissemination, trafficking, or sale of sex-related materials in any form that might be considered socially damaging. Under the Communist regime, the law was very broadly interpreted. Police and court actions would even judge nude pictures as social ills and impose punishments. The criteria for determining the materials' illegality was not specifically stipulated.

Judgment as to the acceptability or not of the materials' characteristics were determined by sexologists and psychologists appointed by a judge for the item's review. Currently, as in the past, particular attention is given to subjects involving sex with children or animals and somehow judged "humiliating to human dignity." The punishments can range from confiscation of the materials and fine or imprisonment of 2–5 years.

Sexual crimes, such as rape, attempted rape, sexual assault, and child sex abuse, are considered major offenses. Sex-related offenses, such as peeping and indecent exposure, are considered of lesser consequence. The Ministry of the Interior maintains data separately on all these types of sex behaviors.

Prior to 2000, only interactions that involved genital-genital heterosexual intercourse were considered rape or attempted rape. From the year 2000, however, changes in the law made it possible to prosecute with the same severity of other cases of sexual violence that could include, for instance, forced or coerced homosexual, anal, or oral intercourse. This thus enhances the potential scope for a higher number of reported sex-related offenses.

Measuring Social Changes and Access to Pornography

Data on the number of crimes reported were obtained from the Ministry of the Interior. These data allowed for a detailed analysis of all sorts of sex-related infractions. Critical comparisons were between the period during which there was a strict prohibition against pornography (before November 1989) and the period following until the end of 2007. Basically, this allowed comparison of a 15–17-year interval during which any pornography was illegal with an 18-year span during which it was widely available. This post-change duration obviously includes the current era of readily obtainable Internet porn.

Accurate and definitive figures for the amounts of types of SEM available during our study periods were not available. In effect, no pornography of any sort was legally available under the Communist regime and policing activities against it then were vigorous. With the switch to democracy, all sorts of porn became easily procured. One index of the availability of published pornography for the post-1989 interval under review was obtained from PK 62 Inc., publishers of SEM holding a majority of market share from its start-up in 1990 until the present. Their records, according to Mr. Pavel Kvoriak, director of PK 62 . . . , indicate a steady and rapid rise in the number of printed copies of pornographic magazines sold in Czechoslovakia and then in the Czech Republic and Slovakia together. Magazine sales exceeded 4 million copies in 1995. After Czechoslovakia split in 1993 sales in the Czech Republic alone were between 80 and 90% of PK 62 Inc. total sales. Their main competitor, MP Media, sold about 30–40% of the amount sold by PK 62. After the year 2000, the sale of pornographic CDs became popular and available. Another index as to the availability of pornography would be the continuing increase in available Internet access from fewer than 5.8% of the households having such connections in 2001 to the 29.9% in

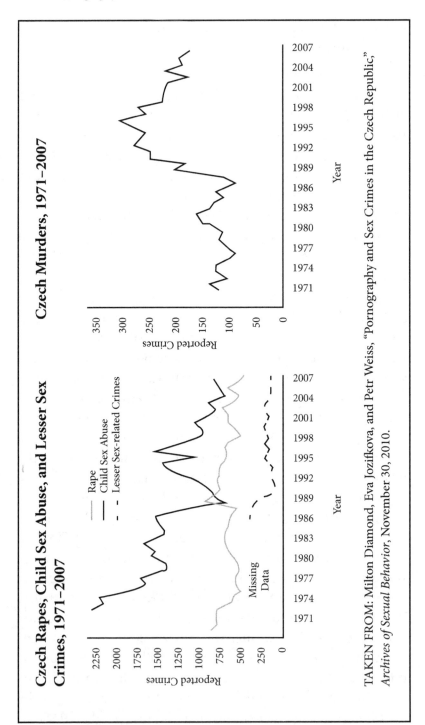

Czech Rapes, Child Sex Abuse, and Lesser Sex Crimes, 1971–2007

Czech Murders, 1971–2007

TAKEN FROM: Milton Diamond, Eva Jozifkova, and Petr Weiss, "Pornography and Sex Crimes in the Czech Republic," *Archives of Sexual Behavior*, November 30, 2010.

2007 (Czech Statistical Office). It can thus safely be assumed, however calculated, that the types and amounts of sex-related SEM publicly available have increased considerably since the change to democracy.

As comparative markers of social change, and for comparison, we also investigated the murder, criminal assault, and robbery figures reported for the corresponding intervals under study. Particularly appropriate for our comparisons, murders and assaults were divided by the Czech police authorities into sex-related (e.g., associated with rape) and non-sex-related categories (e.g., associated with robbery).

A Decrease in Sex Crimes, but an Increase in Violent Crimes

Most obvious and most significant of our findings is that the number of reported cases of child sex abuse immediately dropped markedly after SEM was legalized and became available. The incidence of reported child sex abuse, following this original precipitous decline following the governmental switch in 1989, did increase in incidence for a few years to peak in 1995 and 1998 but then again dropped in number following a downward trend that had begun prior to democratization.

Reported cases of rape did briefly pitch upward following the change to democracy and the availability of pornography but then returned to its frequency seen during the period under communism: between about 500–750 cases a year. Considering the complete post-1989 period, the number of reported rapes did not increase after SEM was legalized. This stability was maintained despite a significant increase in the male population aged 15–64 over the years from 3,225,960 in 1971 to 3,726,148 in 2007. Statistical analysis did not show any correlation between the number of men in the population and the reported cases of rape.

The so-called lesser sexual offenses of indecent exposure, peeping, etc., also decreased significantly following the legal availability of SEM. In comparison with our findings for the sex crimes mentioned following democratization and porn availability, the number of societal crimes of general murder, assault, and robbery rose significantly. Murders associated with robbery or with other non-sex-related motives increased sharply. Murders associated with sex-related matters—small in number at any time—did not increase. The number of reported sex-related crimes decreased significantly from the pre-switch period to the post period, whereas the number of reported nonsexual crimes increased significantly.

Changing Access to Pornography and Changing Attitudes

The most obvious and significant finding is that since 1989, with the shift from a political system with its total ban on SEM and anything that might be considered pornographic to the present regime and the widespread availability of SEM in various media from publication to films, CDs and the Internet, the incidence of reported sex-related crimes has not increased. Perhaps most critically, child sex abuse, despite a brief upswing toward its pre-democracy rate, resumed a decline that had begun, for unknown reasons, in the early 1970s. The lesser sex-related crimes of peeping and indecent exposure also dropped significantly and appears to have reached a low and steady state. This is interesting since child sex abuse and so-called "hands off" sex crimes are supposedly the most resistant to change.

Concurrently, the number of reported rapes and attempted rapes, after an immediate but brief rise following the release from communism and advent of available SEM, returned to their pre-revolution numbers. This occurred despite a significant increase in the male (and female) populations.

Interestingly, at least for the 4 years following the new availability of pornography and governmental change, there is little evidence that the social views against SEM had markedly changed. [P.] Weiss and Weiss and [E.] Zverina surveyed Czech men and women in 1993, 1998, and 2003 regarding their acceptance of pornography. In all three surveys, men were more permissive than women. However, their results showed that, among both men and women, social acceptance of pornographic materials has essentially remained the same; some 50% of both men and women retained reservations about the acceptance of porn despite the dramatic change in circumstances. The only significant sex difference was that more men in all three surveys, approximately 30%, thought SEM should be available without restrictions while only about half as many women felt similarly. According to the 2003 survey, 26% of the women questioned would forbid pornography while only 9% of the men would do so.

It might be said that while social conservatism persisted, personal values changed; this seems indicated by results of a study on teen females aged 16–18 and their sexual behavior. During the period 1986–1989, response to the question of "what was the reasoning that led to first coitus" the most frequent answer was "obliged her partner." By 1994, that response had significantly decreased and the new answer was "wished it for myself."

When Child Pornography Was Legal, Child Sexual Abuse Declined

Significantly, these changes have occurred during a period of nearly two decades, from 1989 to 2007, during which the possession of child pornography was not illegal. At the same time, society could be said to be changing in negative ways as measured by the increase in robbery, impersonal murder, and other general types of crime. And, again in contrast, the number of sexually motivated murders or killings somehow associated with sex did not increase. Thus, the widespread increase in pornography since 1989 did not appear to have any noticeable adverse social effect as measured by any reported increase in sex crimes.

While the rates for reported rape and sex-related assault did not increase, there were indications that post-communism,

Czech society became more sensitive to rape and sex-related crimes. Before the revolution, everything related to sex was hidden and not publicly discussed. Afterward, problems in these areas began to be openly dealt with. Organizations for victim support and general education of the population regarding sexual matters emerged and were established after the revolution. Training increasingly focused on special police details to enhance their ability to communicate with and deal empathically with victims. Such activities were postulated as appropriate for the new democracy period.

It has been suggested that it is quite probable that false accusations may at least partially explain the increase in the number of reported sex abuse crimes after the government changed in 1989. These appear to be associated with an increase in divorce and other indices of social discord. [E.] Mala, [J.] Raboch, and [Z.] Sovak found an increased tendency for advisories in domestic legal disputes to falsely accuse partners of sex crimes after the revolution. These researchers suggest that up to 55% of child sex abuse accusations were false when they occurred in property-dividing disputes or guardianship legal disputes involving child custody. Cases of divorce increased significantly following the switch from communism.

The rebound jump in rape following the dramatic political revolution might also be a phenomenon notably associated with dramatic social change or upheaval. As in times of war, the incidence of rape increases when offenders believe the chaos will hide the incident and authorities have other priorities that demand attention. We believe the disorder that accompanied the political revolution may have, for some, encouraged the same temporary strategy.

Child Sex Trafficking a Result of Capitalism, Not Child Porn

The striking rise in reported child sex abuse depicted for the last half decade of the 1990s, according to notations and records . . . , do not apparently relate to the same types of child sex abuse recorded previously or afterward. They are believed to more closely reflect a concerted effort by the government to deal with a rise in child prostitution and the influx of foreign pimps, their prostitutes, and clients following the introduction of capitalism. This phenomenon seemed to be caused by the new economic situation and the society's attempt to cope. Once the child prostitution surge was dealt with, the downward trend in overall reports of child sex abuse continued.

[T.D.] Kendall conducted an in-depth analysis of possible relationships between society, pornography, rape, and the Internet for the state of California. Kendall found that the arrival of the Internet, while not seeming to have an effect on other crimes, was associated with a reduction in rape incidence. After checking the results for the effects of the extent of porn use, user marital status, size of city in which potential rapists might live, possible economic status, and other social and demographic features, Kendall concluded that "potential rapists perceive pornography as a substitute for rape . . . pornography is a complement for masturbation or consensual sex, which themselves are substitutes for rape, making pornography a net substitute for rape." This conclusion reflects on the earlier findings of [M.] Goldstein et al. These investigators, having extensively interviewed and surveyed rapists, pedophiles, and others along with control groups of persons with no history of sex offenses about their use of pornography, found that sex-offender and sex-deviate groups not only have had less experience with pornography but when they do come across it ". . . report a higher incidence of masturbation in response to erotic materials than the controls." They go on to conclude that "the erotic materials are much more significant in producing masturbatory reaction in the users compared with the controls than in inducing sexual relations."

It is also noteworthy that the number of paraphilias (e.g., indecent exposure) decreased significantly following the ready availability of SEM. Usually such activities are considered relatively refractive to change. Here again, we believe potential infractions in this regard were prevented by the simple expedient of masturbation. We believe our findings support the displacement function of pornography for potential sex offenders.

Issues surrounding child pornography and child sex abuse are probably among the most contentious in the area of sex issues and crime. In this regard, we consider instructive our findings for the Czech Republic that have echoed those found in Denmark and Japan that where so-called child pornography was readily available without restriction the incidence of child sexual abuse was lower than when its availability was restricted. As with adult pornography appearing to substitute for sexual aggression everywhere it has been investigated, we believe the availability of child porn does similarly. We believe this particularly since the findings of Weiss have shown that a substantial portion of child sex abuse instances seemed to occur not because of pedophilic interest of the abuser, but because the child was used as a substitute subject.

The Link Between Child Pornography and Child Abuse

We do not approve of the use of real children in the production or distribution of child pornography but artificially produced materials might serve. As it is, with restrictions on even materials for the scientific study of the phenomenon forbidden to all but police enforcement agencies, these real-life studies are the only way to begin to understand the phenomenon. Unfortunately, we do not have a breakdown by age of the perpetrators or victims of sex abuse. With the new Czech Republic law against child pornography, however, analysis of findings over the next 5–10 years could show if this new prohibition against child pornography is correlated with an increase or decrease in sex crimes against children or without any noticeable effect.

Important to note are recent findings by Swiss investigators that viewing child pornography does not seem to be a risk factor for future sex offenses. These investigators checked recidivism rates for "hands-on" child sex offenders with porn-viewing-only offenders and concluded "consuming child pornography alone is not a risk factor for committing hands-on sex offenses. . . . The majority of the investigated consumers had no previous convictions for hands-on sex offenses. For those offenders, the prognosis for hands-on sex offenses, as well as for recidivism with child pornography, is favorable."

Periodical and Internet Sources Bibliography

The following articles have been selected to supplement the diverse views presented in this chapter.

David Aaronovitch   "Don't Look Now: In the Sordid World of Child Abuse, Fantasy and Reality Are Perilously Intertwined," *Observer*, January 19, 2003.

BBC News   "Child Abuse Image Trade Targeted," BBC News, March 3, 2009.

Ken Blackwell and Ken Klukowski   "Child Porn at MTV," *American Spectator*, January 26, 2011.

Chris Calabrese   "We Must Combat Child Pornography Without Abandoning Online Privacy," *ACLU Blog of Rights*, May 26, 2011. www.aclu.org/blog.

Siobhan Courtney   "Pornographic Videos Flood YouTube," BBC News, May 21, 2009.

Paulo Fagundes   "Fighting Internet Child Pornography—The Brazilian Experience," *Police Chief*, September 2009.

Chateau Heartiste (blog)   "Want Fewer Sex Crimes? Legalize Victimless Sexual Outlets," *Chateau Heartiste* (blog), December 2, 2010. https://heartiste.wordpress .com.

Jim Hu   "Court Strikes Down Pennsylvania Porn Law," CNET News, September 10, 2004. http://news .cnet.com.

Ian Urbina   "Court Rejects Law Limiting Online Pornography," *New York Times*, March 23, 2007.

CHAPTER 4

Can Online Pornography Be Regulated?

Chapter Preface

Emotions tend to run high in debates about online pornography, where the discourse tends to be divided in broad strokes: women's rights and safety vs. freedom of speech; protecting children vs. respecting adults' privacy; cultural decay vs. open-mindedness. What tends to disappear in the debate are simple questions like: Even if we could agree that pornography should be banned from the Internet, could we accomplish that? This question has ever-expanding implications, both political and technological.

On the political front, US-based online pornography is no more regulated, by and large, than any other film, photography, or web-based publication business. The tools to run such a business are nearly universally accessible: Almost every cell phone in America can shoot photos or videos and upload them to the Internet. Enforcing a ban on producing and distributing pornography even within US borders would be challenging. And, although the bulk of online pornography currently appears to be produced in the United States, an increasing portion—especially in the world of sexually explicit online chat—originates in eastern Europe, Africa, and Asia. Banning online pornography would, at the least, seem to call for the sort of international multilateral cooperation that no issue in recent history—from the war on terror to drug interdiction to preventing human trafficking or genocide—has been able to inspire.

Technologically, the prognosis is even more dire. The Internet itself—a distributed network of computers, each able to communicate with any other point on the network—was conceived and built as a military communications system and university research tool over the course of the 1970s and 1980s. It was designed to be, first and foremost, a robust system able to maintain its integrity even as nodes unpredictably joined and disappeared—as might be the case following a natural disaster, act of war, or as a consequence of any of the mundane power fluctuations or equipment outages that regularly plagued poorly funded university programs. The Internet's core goal was to maintain the network itself, automatically patching any holes as they appeared. As John Gilmore, an American computer scientist and cofounder of the Electronic Frontier Foundation, has famously quipped, "The Net interprets censorship as damage and routes around it." Interestingly, Gilmore's observation was made in response to a question about online pornography, as quoted in a 1993 *Time* magazine article:

> Unlike the family-oriented commercial services, which censor messages they find offensive, the Internet imposes no restrictions. Anybody can start a discussion on any topic and say anything. There have been sporadic attempts by local network managers to crack down on the raunchier discussion groups, but as Internet pioneer John Gilmore puts it, "The Net interprets censorship as damage and routes around it."

> The casual visitor to the newsgroups on the Usenet (a bulletin-board system that began as a competitor to the Internet but has been largely subsumed by it) will discover discussion groups labeled, according to the Net's idiosyncratic cataloging system, alt.sex.masturbation, alt.sex.bondage and alt.sex.fetish.feet. On Internet Relay Chat, a global 24-hour-a-day message board, one can stumble upon imaginary orgies played out with one-line typed commands ("Now I'm taking off your shirt . . ."). In alt.binaries.pictures.erotica, a user can peek at snapshots that would make a sailor blush.

And although much has changed since 1993—both in terms of consumer technology for accessing the Internet, and the fundamental infrastructure that forms its backbone—the fundamental things still apply: The Internet is a porous, cooperative network eager to shuffle bytes from point A to point B, and entirely uninterested in what those bytes might add up to.

The following chapter attempts to answer the questions—perhaps the most important queries in the entire debate about Internet pornography—of whether online pornography should be, and can be, regulated.

"Right now . . . you have just two options: Give up the Internet or give in to its seedy underbelly. That's a choice that parents should not have to make."

Online Porn Can and Should Be Regulated

Chuck Schumer

Chuck Schumer is the senior Democratic US senator representing the state of New York. Schumer is widely admired for his ability to build consensus, especially on contentious issues. In his 2007 book Positively American: Winning Back the Middle-Class Majority One Family at a Time, *Schumer devotes a chapter to online pornography, and how lax regulation and enforcement make it all too accessible to children. According to Schumer, online pornography viewed in the United States—regardless of its origin—should be regulated through credit card payment processors, which are much more responsive to government intervention than the vast number of pornography webmasters.*

As you read, consider the following questions:

1. What are the stipulations of Chuck Schumer's 2003 CAN-SPAM legislation?

2. What are the two key aspects of Schumer's plan to control minors' access to online pornography through credit card processors?

3. The senator suggests that cell phone contracts and the packaging of other web-accessible entertainment devices should include an informational box, similar to the "Schumer Box" on credit card statements. What would Senator Schumer like to see printed on these cell phone and iPod "Schumer Boxes"?

In college, I had a friend who was a radical. When I joined the Harvard Young Democrats, she scoffed. She did not believe in working within the system; she believed in working against it. While I was organizing letter-writing campaigns arguing against the war in Vietnam to members of Congress, she was at Walpole State Prison counseling inmates on how to run the prison when the guards went on strike.

A Radical Liberal Takes on Internet Pornography

Throughout college, we would argue all the time. Sometimes I felt like we talked for only two reasons: So she could yell at me about something I was doing or see the shock on my face when she told me about something she was doing.

From time to time, my phone would ring at 7 a.m. I would groggily answer.

"Chuck," I would hear through static. "I hitchhiked to Northfield."

"You what?" I would scream.

"I'll be here a day or two. There's a poetry reading."

"Don't you have a test tomorrow?"

"I don't know. Maybe. Don't tell anyone, okay? 'Bye."

Now my old friend lives in the suburbs and has two great kids. But she is still more liberal than this old square. On many mornings I have come into my Senate office to find that she's sent me a newspaper clipping. I always hope it's an article from the local *Bee* about her life or her children or, heaven forbid, a piece about an issue I've been working on. But more often than not, I'll find an op-ed by Paul Krugman, an editorial from the *Nation* or a long academic treatise. The same note is always typed neatly at the top:

Chuck,

DO SOMETHING ABOUT THIS!!!

Hope you're well.

The Internet Brings Pornography Home

Over the last couple of years, the subject of the clips has changed. She less often highlights concerns about the spotted owl or complains about violations of Title IX's gender-equity provisions. Now, one of her main causes is Internet pornography. You see, stopping the spread of pornography on the Internet has become her number one cause. Although she might not know it, for once my friend is on the same page as Joe and Eileen Bailey [a fictional middle-class family].

The Baileys use the Internet. Joe used it to research cars when the old Taurus finally gave out. Eileen keeps up with the kids' soccer schedules by e-mail. But the three Bailey kids spend a lot more time on the computer than either of their parents do. They send e-mails, they search the Web, they have MySpace profiles. Pete's face lights up when he finds a new Web page about magic tricks; Abby's friends from day camp stay in touch with a weekly online chat. Joe and Eileen encourage this—they know that having Internet skills will be critical as their kids get older—but it also makes them uneasy.

Because let's face it, for all the virtuous things the Internet has brought into our homes, it has also brought pornography.

The porn industry grosses roughly $12 billion per year—more than ABC, NBC and CBS combined. There are 420 million pages of Internet pornography on the Web. Nearly one out of every eight Web sites is pornographic! Today, the most frequent viewers of online pornography are kids between the ages of twelve and seventeen. The typical eleven-year-old has seen Internet pornography.

More Extreme and More Common than Yesterday's Girly Magazines

Of course, pornography has been around since people sketched figures in caves. When Joe Bailey was growing up, he probably had his first experience with it at the local malt shop. As he headed for the counter at the back of the store, he would cast a guilty glance at the dirty magazines partially shrouded on the top row of the magazine rack. Or when he was thirteen, maybe he raced through a tattered *Playboy* that a buddy found in the neighbor's trash can.

Today, pornography has changed. With the click of a mouse, it is possible for children to be exposed to images that most adults a generation ago would not have seen throughout their whole lives. And these images are making their way into middle schools and high schools. More and more often, kids are imitating what they see.

We need to make it harder for kids to access pornographic sites. Today's blocking software is not good enough. Kids have a better chance of installing blocking software correctly—and then disabling it—than their parents do. In a lot of families, parents can't get blocking programs to work without their kids' help. The thin veil separating the Bailey children from the coarse and dark world of online porn is nothing more substantial than a simple Web search and the click of a mouse.

Pornography Enters the Schumer Home

Iris and I learned just how big a problem online pornography is a few years ago, when we set up an AOL e-mail account for Jessica and Alison. I figured that our teenage girls would use their account to talk about homework or dissect the results of last week's CYO Basketball League game. I did have one concern—I told Iris they might use it to correspond with boys from school.

Iris laughed at me. "Yeah, Chuck, they might."

Jessica and Alison laughed at me. "Yeah, Dad, we might."

As often happens in our house, the women prevailed.

But before long, the in-box was full of notices about opportunities to invest in Nigerian oil wells, pitches about buying cheap prescription drugs (if only it were so easy!) and, to our horror, explicit advertisements for pornographic Web sites.

No one in our house had ever expressed interest in Nigerian energy futures, black-market pharmaceuticals or pornographic Web sites. All we had done was create an e-mail account that somehow got harvested by a spam e-mail ring. Through the Internet, pornography was creeping into our house. And there was nothing we could do to stop it.

That's when I started proposing legislation to do something about spam. In 2003, working with Senator Conrad Burns, Senator Ron Wyden and the Commerce Committee, we passed CAN-SPAM. CAN-SPAM is what we call the Controlling the Assault of Non-Solicited Pornography and Marketing Act—members of Congress have a weakness for acronyms.

Stopping Porn Spam

CAN-SPAM makes it a crime to send unidentified commercial e-mails, requires clear identification of sexually explicit e-mail and mandates that all commercial e-mails have an opt-out reply option.

Mainly due to blocking software developed by e-mail providers, but partially because of CAN-SPAM, it's no longer the Wild West when it comes to spam. Quantifying the total volume of spam is difficult, but there's no question that many users have seen a marked decrease. Still, without better enforcement, the problem will not be solved.

But even more important than defeating spam is blocking kids' access to the porn sites themselves. As I've said, they're huge and they're everywhere. Their presence casts a shadow across the entire Internet. Teens know all about them and, too often, have no trouble gaining access to them.

The solution here must be smart. Many pornographers are shady, underground figures. They will happily go offshore rather than be held accountable for their sites' content. They won't cut down on kids' access to adult sites voluntarily or out of a sense of decency.

Porn purveyors, almost by definition, aren't worried about decency or discretion. They want money. If we can cut off their funding, we can force them to comply with the law, and in that way protect kids from their product.

Controlling Online Porn Payment

Since porn companies often elude enforcement by going offshore and underground, we must focus on the involved parties who can't—the credit card companies and Internet payment processing services. These are the lifelines that keep the shady world of Internet pornography afloat; the money collected by credit card companies and payment services is everything to pornographers. And, unlike Web site operators, MasterCard, Visa and American Express can't disappear. They can't go offshore.

And, unlike Web operators, they can be compelled to comply with the law.

A bill offered by Senator Blanche Lincoln of Arkansas would apply some much-needed regulation to this multibillion-dollar industry. Blanche is a wonderful mother and a wonderful senator. The Lincoln bill would hold credit card companies, banks and other Internet payment processing companies responsible for the money they collect on behalf of Internet pornographers.

It is counterproductive to regulate porn Web sites that operate within our borders but to, in effect, give carte blanche to those that go offshore. The Lincoln bill would allow us to regulate all pay pornography sites, no matter what shelter these sleazebags burrow into.

Age Verification and Taxation

Credit card companies and payment services should be forbidden from processing transactions for any Web sites that do not comply with rules designed to make the Internet safe for children. The first rule is reliable age verification. All pornographic Web sites should require users to verify their age with a government-approved ID, such as a driver's license, that matches a credit card. The Web sites should also be required to use age-verification software that has no loopholes and has been approved by the Federal Trade Commission (FTC). Financial institutions would be allowed to take payments only for Web sites that complied. Those that didn't comply, or gave kids access to porn, would be fined an amount far more than the cost of doing business. This would significantly increase the barriers to entering a pornography site—instead of merely clicking "Yes, I am 18," perhaps dishonestly, unlawful entry would require full-fledged ID theft.

The second new regulation should be a 25% excise tax on the sale of Internet pornography. As with age-verification requirements, the onus would be on payment processors to collect these taxes. The money would be put in a trust fund and used to catch child pornographers and child predators, monitor age verification, develop better blocking software, show parents and teachers how to monitor children's online activity and truly enforce CAN-SPAM. CAN-SPAM has taught us that you need serious resources to enforce the law on the Internet. The trust fund would finally give the chronically underfunded FTC the resources it needs to track down international rings hell-bent on breaking the law.

The key here is to put adult Web sites out of the reach of kids by holding financial institutions' feet to the fire. The credit card companies and payment processing services are making a significant profit through processing Internet porn. Unlike the porn providers, they are aboveground and can be forced to comply with the law. It is only fair to hold them accountable.

As with so many solutions in this book, rational enforcement to stop those who brazenly break the law is one part of the equation. Providing better information that will give the Baileys the tools they need to protect their kids and themselves is the other.

Transparency for Consumers

I have always believed that giving consumers more information is the key to making the market work. That's why I created the Schumer Box for credit cards—to make critical information accessible and clear. The Schumer Box pulls important fee and interest-rate information out of the small print and puts it in plain sight on every credit card contract. You used to need a corporate lawyer and a magnifying glass to know what you were getting into when you signed up for a new card. Joe and Eileen don't have the time or the money for that. But if they can see their options set out clearly, they will decide what works best for them.

We must give consumers the same easily accessible information on how to deal with pornography. Many parents don't realize it, but cell phones and other new gadgets also give kids access to the dark world of porn. Although CAN-SPAM made it illegal to send pornographic spam to cell phones, we must do more to stop it. Cell phone contracts should include an informational box that warns parents that their kids can access pornography and provides information on how to use blocking technology to prevent it. This requirement should apply to makers of portable entertainment devices like iPods, as well.

This sort of government intervention—prohibiting exploitative commercial activity and providing useful information to help people protect themselves—is exactly what the Baileys want. Joe and Eileen don't believe in overly restrictive regulation. If they were asked about it, they might say that they don't want all adult content to be banned; they would resent the government making their choices for them. But they want a government that can keep companies honest and that makes it easier to make informed choices. They also believe that kids don't, and shouldn't, have the same rights that adults do. When the government steps in to keep kids from accessing pornography, they applaud.

Right now, unless you're a computer expert, you have just two options: Give up the Internet or give in to its seedy underbelly. That's a choice that parents should not have to make.

For once, my old friend from college is not asking for something that's all that radical. All that she, and Joe and Eileen, need is tools that will let her control what comes into her living room. Targeted regulation, strong enforcement and clear disclosure will give us the tools we need to protect kids.

All while letting Pete Bailey find all the magic tricks a twenty-first-century kid could ever want.

> *"Once the infrastructure for filtering is in place—for any reason, though porn is usually the first excuse—there is an incentive to increase its use."*

Online Pornography Should Not Be Regulated

Krishna Rau

Krishna Rau is a Canadian journalist who frequently writes about youth sexuality and homosexual issues, often for Xtra! Canada's Gay and Lesbian News. *In the following viewpoint, Rau explores the ramifications of bans, both legal and voluntary, on pornographic material. Rau warns of the tendency for "mission creep," whereby legal or technological limitations placed on one type of material, such as pornographic images, are then employed to stifle what was previously considered legitimate—if not necessarily universally enjoyed—personal expression or political speech.*

As you read, consider the following questions:

1. According to the Electronic Frontier Foundation (EFF), what problems arise when Internet service providers "voluntarily" comply with government pressure, rather than waiting for actual legal statutes to be enacted?

2. Why is non-pornographic gay and lesbian web content often blocked by "porn" filters?

3. Nart Villeneuve identifies four issues with porn-blocking software. What are they?

For most people sex and the Internet are as natural a pairing as apple pie and motherhood.

But increasingly the easy access to pornography that so many have enjoyed for so long is being regulated, filtered and censored by a combination of government, law enforcement, Internet service providers (ISPs) and moral busybodies.

At the Edge of a Slippery Slope

Free speech activists say what we're seeing now is the beginning of Internet censorship, with the regulation and removal of child porn as the initial motivation.

"There are efforts to combat images of the sexual abuse of prepubescent children and the major ISPs are involved," says Nart Villeneuve, a research fellow at the University of Toronto's Citizen Lab—which has done work with Chinese bloggers and dissidents on how to avoid Internet censorship—in an e-mail. "They filter access to a small amount of sites that host this stuff and have review/complaint procedures and do not appear to be overblocking.

"But once the infrastructure for filtering is in place—for any reason, though porn is usually the first excuse—there is an incentive to increase its use. I see 'mission creep' all the time where once in place, filtering is extended to cover content areas that were not in the original mandate."

Chris Hansen, a staff lawyer with the American Civil Liberties Union (ACLU), agrees that we're at the beginning of that very slippery slope.

"I don't think the people who are trying to get rid of child porn are going after other types of speech," he says. "But I do think they are willing to take steps in the name of suppressing child porn that has the effect of suppressing other types of speech. There are those who believe the safest approach is to eliminate everything.

"What sort of collateral damage are we willing to accept?"

"Voluntary" Business Solutions Void First Amendment Rights

That sort of massive overkill has already been displayed by several governments in the US. New York State has already pressured major ISPs to shut down Usenet groups, which still make up a large chunk of online newsgroups.

"New York attorney general Andrew Cuomo recently succeeded in pressuring AOL and AT&T to join the ranks of Verizon, Sprint and Time Warner Cable in limiting access to many or all of the Usenet newsgroups hosted on their servers," said an article from the Electronic Frontier Foundation (EFF) in July [2008]. "This tactic will hinder free speech and the access to information in Usenet communities, without deterring the child pornographer. But since the ISPs are 'voluntarily' bowing to political pressure, rather than obeying a statutory edict, traditional First Amendment court challenges are unlikely to protect these online communities."

According to the EFF, "An investigation found 88 groups containing child pornography, or 0.5 percent of the active discussion groups in the alt.* hierarchy. Verizon and Sprint are taking down one gigantic subset of groups, the very popular alt.* hierarchy. AT&T will block all alt.binaries.* groups, while Time Warner Cable and AOL are shutting down their Usenet service entirely."

The alt.* groups contain newsgroups on sexuality, porn and other "alternative" topics.

Jerry Brown, California's attorney general, has asked ISPs in his state to follow the same procedures.

Hansen says that while such decisions are regrettable ACLU will not take on private business decisions.

"Number two. That's the art that offended me."

"Number two. That's the art that offended me," cartoon by Mike Baldwin. www.cartoonstock.com. Copyright © Mike Baldwin. Reproduction rights obtainable from www.CartoonStock.com.

"ISPs are not under any obligation to carry anything," he says. "For an ISP to say it will not carry Playboy.com does not raise any civil liberties issues."

American decisions also have an impact in Canada. In 2006 Montreal-based ISP Epifora was told by MCI Canada, which hosted its connection to the Internet, that a number of the groups on Epifora were in violation of the "acceptable use policy" of Verizon, MCI's owner.

The alleged violations centred around such sites as Boy-Chat and GirlChat, which were self-described at the time as "self-help message boards for minor-attracted adults," and a website run by John Robin Sharpe, who was unsuccessfully prosecuted for child porn.

Although Epifora asked the police to review their sites, and were told they were legal, the ISP was forced to find another host. Epifora went out of business in 2007, according to the *Montreal Gazette*.

Police Access to Personal Information

It's the law—and specifically police access to ISP information—that will be one of the next major battles.

Hansen says that in the [United] States nobody is sure what kind of access law enforcement has.

"To what extent do they have access or to what extent are they lawfully allowed to?" he asks. "In either case the answer is we don't know. The government is asserting brand-new powers to listen to anything in the wake of [the terrorist attacks of] 9/11 [September 11, 2001]. The extent to which the police are doing this is unclear. My assumption is the ISPs are cooperating."

In Canada the situation is theoretically more clear. Under Canadian law police must obtain judicial authorization except in cases where they have reason to believe someone is in imminent danger or in certain cases involving foreign intelligence. However ISPs can choose to provide police with subscriber information, they just don't have to.

But there are efforts from all three major national parties to change that.

Political Initiatives in Canada

In 2007 the Conservative government held consultations on proposed legislation that would have given police immediate access to customer names and addresses (CNA).

According to a paper on the Public Safety Canada website, "Law enforcement agencies have been experiencing difficulties in consistently obtaining basic CNA information from tele-communications service providers (TSPs).

"Some companies provide this information voluntarily, while others require a warrant before providing any information, regardless of its nature or the nature of the situation. If the custodian of the information is not cooperative when a request for such information is made, law enforcement agencies may have no means to compel the production of information pertaining to the customer."

Both the Liberals and NDP [New Democratic Party] have put forward similar proposals. The Liberal government put forward legislation in November 2005 which died when an election was called.

That bill, according to the Canadian Internet Policy and Public Interest Clinic, would have allowed police to "obtain specified 'subscriber data' (name, address, telephone number, e-mail address, IP address) upon request from TSPs. . . . Judicial authorization would not be required; TSPs would be obliged to provide the information upon request, without any justification on the part of the law enforcement agency. Moreover TSPs will not be allowed to disclose any information about these requests."

The bill also required providers to have the means of interception built into their system.

NDP MP [member of Parliament] Peter Stoffer put forward a private member's bill in 2007 that would have required ISPs to monitor the activities of their clients, and would hold them criminally and financially responsible for any illegal material posted online by those clients.

"What's the cost of protecting our children, of protecting society?" Stoffer told *Xtra!* last year. "The privacy advocates can go pound sand as far as I'm concerned. I have two young children. We should do everything in our power to protect children. I don't believe in capital punishment, but I'm willing to make an exception. If it was my children, you wouldn't have to worry about the law."

Credit Card Companies Refusing to Work with Porn Sites

But even if your local police, government and ISPs all leave your computer alone, you might still have problems accessing your favourite porn sites.

There's growing pressure on credit card and billing companies to refuse to work with porn sites. The prime example is the American company First Data, a multibillion-dollar IT [information technology] processing company. In 2004 First Data stopped processing transactions for iBill, the company through which millions pay for their porn.

First Data also owns Western Union, which this year cut off services for two businesses owned by Pink Triangle Press, the publisher of *Xtra!* The company refused to accept cash payments for Cruiseline, a phone service which allows men to meet other men for sex, and Squirt, which is a cruising website which also allows users to access gay porn.

"In general terms we do not do business with agencies that engage in adult services," Western Union spokesperson Daniel Diaz told *Xtra!* "We do not allow any explicit content of any kind, photography, subscription-based adult services or other products deemed to be adult services."

Filters Block Non-Pornographic Gay and Lesbian Content

And then there's the question of content filters, which block Internet access to sites deemed unacceptable. Parents, businesses, governments can all use filters to prevent surfers from accessing sites, even in public places like airport lounges or on free public Wi-Fi, which a number of North American cities have experimented with.

Queer content often gets caught up in such filters, even if it isn't the primary target, says Villeneuve.

"Gay and lesbian is often classified as pornography even when there's zero porn on the site," he says. "There's often a lifestyle category that's a euphemism for gay and lesbian. These filtering products often have a very conservative bias. It's quite common in companies or where there's semipublic access."

Villeneuve says the makers of censorship programs rarely reveal the lists or terms they use. On Macs—which block access to Xtra.ca in the Porter Airlines lounge at the Toronto island airport—a user can't find what method Apple uses to decide what sites to censor via its parental controls.

It's that sort of secrecy that's most frightening as ISPs, police and government move toward an online world where we won't even know when we're being censored or watched or who's doing it.

"The big issues concerning blocking pornography, on public Wi-Fi for example, are transparency (do you know when you are blocked?) and accountability (who chooses what to block/unblock?)," writes Villeneuve in an e-mail. "How is content classified and who does it (a filtering company?). Is there a complaint/review mechanism?

"But the most important is the slippery slope: What about artistic nude photos or sexual education? Will a video demonstrating the correct use of a condom be blocked?"

Porn Should Be Restricted to Its Own Internet Domain

Nick Clark

Nick Clark is an arts correspondent for the Independent. *In the following viewpoint, Clark argues that the recent approval of an .xxx domain for pornographic Internet content is a win-win scenario, both for the adult entertainment industry and for consumers. The new domain will be lucrative for business, Clark insists, by providing a quick way for consumers to identify responsible adult content online. The new domain will also benefit consumers trying to avoid pornography altogether, as an .xxx domain will quickly expose website content. Pornography is here to stay, Nick Clark argues, and the new .xxx domain will help provide a way to manage pornographic Internet content.*

As you read, consider the following questions:

1. Why does the author refer to the .xxx domain as an "Internet's red-light district"?

Nick Clark, ".XXX Rated: Internet's Red-Light District Has Arrived," *Independent*, September 7, 2011, p. 44. Copyright © 2011 by Independent Print Ltd. All rights reserved. Reproduced by permission.

2. Why, according to the author, did ICM sign a contract with McAfee to scan all of the .xxx sites?

3. According to the author, why were some adult entertainment companies opposed to the .xxx domain?

Stuart Lawley is expecting a gold rush—and xxx marks the spot. Following a decadelong battle, his company has been given the go-ahead to set up a new sponsored top-level domain targeting the adult entertainment industry. Despite the approval of .xxx the controversy, predictably, has raged on.

ICM Registry, which is based in Florida's Palm Beach and run by Mr Lawley, is overseeing the .xxx domain registration and today is a significant step towards the emergence of thousands of sites with the evocative three letter suffix. From this morning companies and brand owners will have a 50-day "sunrise" period to bid for their own piece of real estate in what has been dubbed the "Internet's red-light district". Both adult entertainment companies and those worried about their reputation can apply to pick up their own brands.

A Responsible Approach to Adult Internet Content

Mr Lawley said that while several .xxx sites had gone live as part of the founders programme, today marked the "proper opening of the doors of the registry". In the not-too-distant future, he expects there to be close to half a million .xxx sites.

ICM said the new domain was created "to promote a responsible approach to adult content on the Internet and offer clear signposts to its locations online". The first to go live with the new domain name was Casting.xxx early last month [August 2011] and since then a further 1,500 sites have been approved. Mr Lawley called it a "win, win, win" development for the industry pointing to benefits for porn consumers, those providing the content and those who wanted to avoid it altogether.

For those that want to avoid porn altogether .xxx will leave Internet users "in no doubt about the underlying content of the sites," he added.

ICM first applied to register the .xxx domain in 2000 but Mr Lawley admitted there was little real hope it would be approved by Icann [Internet Corporation for Assigned Names and Numbers], the not-for-profit corporation that oversees the Internet's naming system, at that stage. It applied again in 2004, but Mr Lawley said, "the US government and the Christian Right became enraged".

Setting Up a New Domain

It would be engaged in costly legal battles for another six years, but Icann finally approved .xxx last year—although three of the 16 board members opposed the move and four abstained. After its approval, there were 900,000 requests lodged for 650,000 unique names. "The phone has been ringing off the hook," Mr Lawley said.

After the "sunrise" period closes, there will be a "land rush" from 8 November giving adult businesses premium access to the remaining sites; 17 days later it will become a free-for-all. ICM's conservative estimates were of 150,000 sites, but Mr Lawley said: "I think it will be closer to 500,000". Interest from consumers was also initially high. Traffic to Casting.xxx spiked in August, briefly overtaking Sex.com, according to data from Internet tracking site Alexa, although its popularity has waned.

Mr Lawley said it reflected trends that the adult industry was trying to regulate itself and confirmed it as an early adopter of technology. "From the VCR and the Camcorder to the Internet the adult industry has always been quick to take up new technology and trends," he said.

Porn sites have a bad reputation for spreading viruses and malware—although Mr Lawley said there was little firm evidence to back this up—but to encourage visits to .xxx sites,

Six Steps to Containing Online Pornography in Its Own Domain

1 Pass legislation setting a deadline for all website operators containing pornographic content on their website to transition their pornographic content from any current TLDs [top-level domain] such as .com or .net to the .XXX TLD if they wish to display this pornographic content in the United States.

2 Pass legislation creating a new tax to be assessed on all revenues generated from U.S.-based pornographic websites to help support the development of a new screening organization.

3 Pass legislation to develop an organization supported by the new tax to help screen websites for pornographic content and issue fines for noncomplying U.S.-based website operators. This same organization can also be in charge of issuing notices of termination to hosting providers for noncomplying U.S.-based website operators.

4 Pass legislation requiring the new organization to create and maintain an international pornographic block list that identifies and contains any non-U.S.-based pornographic websites. . . .

5 Pass legislation requiring all U.S.-based ISPs [Internet service providers] to provide their customers with the option of blocking the .XXX TLD at the ISP level. In addition, this legislation will require all U.S.-based ISPs to block all websites contained on the international pornographic block list at the ISP level.

6 Create a community of supporters to help screen websites for pornographic content and refer noncomplying websites to the new screening organization.

"BlockXXX.org Flow Chart for Change,"
BlockXXX.org, June 6, 2011. http://blockxxx.org.

ICM has signed a contract with McAfee, the Internet security company, to scan all of the .xxx sites.

Mr Lawley added that the adult industry would benefit as it will ensure "responsible adult content is easily identified on-line, leading to greater and more predictable revenues". Yet several have reacted angrily to the prospect of having to pay to register their site with a .xxx domain or face losing it to a competitor. Mr Lawley said that complaints have been the exception, with the majority of the industry welcoming .xxx.

ICM has spent close to $20m getting to this point, but hopes it can raise somewhere close to $30m in its first year. The company sets its rate at $60 a year and has made close to $4m from its founders programme. The sites have to be sold through registers who vary their pricing. Go Daddy charges $99 a year while Domainmonster charges $77. Dan Cryan, a senior analyst at IHS Screen Digest, expressed doubts over the importance of .xxx. He pointed out there was plenty of porn available already on the web, a trend that would not change. "This seems to be primarily a marketing ploy. It may make some sense for established brands," he said.

Jerry Barnett, the managing director of Strictly Anywhere, which has rebranded to Anywhere.xxx, agreed: "This won't make or break a business but it will be a useful marketing tool."

Mr Barnett, who is also a member of the council that will set the rules for .xxx domains, said it was "nice to have a new namespace. It is reminiscent of the '90s when you could still pick up decent domain names".

Mr Lawley said: "Porn is not going away, and doesn't want to operate in the shadows. This will change the face of the adult industry, it will become an increasingly accepted part of the fabric of the Internet."

A Unique Source of Embarrassment

While porn companies expressed mixed feelings over the approval of .xxx sites, the news was met with dismay by many outside the adult entertainment industry. This prompted ICM Registry to allow companies to block such sites associated with their names, the only domain to allow such a move.

ICM chief executive Stuart Lawley said the company was, "sensitive to non-industry brand owners who do not want their trademarks associated with adult content".

The "sunrise" period offers trademark owners to apply to opt out of the registry, "enabling businesses to be proactive in avoiding brand conflicts". The companies will still have to pay about $200 to cover the costs of removing their names.

Douglas Thomson, trademark attorney with the law firm Marks & Clerk, said cybersquatting—where others buy up names in the hope of selling them on or linking to other sites—was a problem across the web "but has the potential for uniquely embarrassing and damaging consequences in this case". He cautioned: "Nonetheless there is a danger that trademark owners could miss this opportunity. The only sure way to protect their brands cheaply is by blocking them from the .XXX domain."

ICM has already removed potential sites linked to celebrity names including beyonce.xxx, angelinajolie.xxx as well as political figures including Barack Obama and David Cameron.

"Porn and mainstream businesses alike complain they are being forced to buy domain names they don't want, don't need and won't use."

Porn Should Not Be Restricted to Its Own Internet Domain

Terry Baynes

Terry Baynes is a reporter for news organizations such as the on-line business newspaper International Business Times. *In the following viewpoint, he explores the launch of .xxx—a new porn-specific, top-level Internet domain—and the growing resistance against it. According to Baynes, both porn and mainstream companies are buying .xxx websites they complain they "don't want, don't need and won't use" to protect existing brands. Some companies, he reports, have compared the process to blackmail. Most mainstream companies purchasing .xxx websites, such as MTV Networks, are purchasing them only to block others from using the websites. Restricting pornography to its own Internet domain is causing more problems than it's worth, Baynes concludes.*

As you read, consider the following questions:

1. What is the name of the private company that is introducing .xxx?

2. What are cybersquatters, according to the author?

3. According to the author, why do nonprofits such as the Red Cross receive "special treatment"?

In preparation for a new triple-x Internet domain that will launch in December [2011], lawyers for the most storied brands in the United States are scrambling to prevent an x-rated rip-off of an invaluable asset: corporate Web addresses.

Protecting Existing Brands

The domain operator administering the .xxx domain is accepting early applications from brand owners who want control over their names. ICM Registry says it has received over 900,000 "expressions of interest" from companies that want to preregister their trademarks or block others from snapping them up to create, say, a Barbie.xxx or Coke.xxx.

While some adult-content providers are paying the approximately $200 fee because they want to use the domain, other non-porn brands ranging from MTV Networks and Budget Travel to the Red Cross are preregistering to avoid future legal battles with cybersquatters who register trademarks with the intention of reselling them.

Porn and mainstream businesses alike complain they are being forced to buy domain names they don't want, don't need and won't use—and compare the process to a holdup.

"Many feel they're being blackmailed to protect their brands," said Kristina Rosette, a trademark lawyer at the law firm Covington & Burling. She added that requiring preregistration fees to protect trademarks is not uncommon among domain registries, which then include the expected revenue in their business plans and projections.

ICM Registry, the private company that is introducing .xxx, was founded by Stuart Lawley, a British tech investor. He and his partners first proposed the .xxx domain in 2000 to the Internet Corporation for Assigned Names and Numbers (ICANN), the international governing body that oversees top-level domains and reviews new applications. Yet because of fierce opposition from religious and conservative groups on moral grounds, and the Internet pornography industry, which feared censorship, it took ICM until this past March to win a final approval from ICANN's board and a 10-year contract to manage the .xxx domain.

Not Making a Dime

Now that Lawley is finally in the homestretch and preparing to launch ICM in December, he dismisses charges that he is shaking down registrants. "We're doing it on a cost-recovery basis. We don't make a dime out of it," he said, adding that the fees would serve to cover the cost of verifying the applicant's identity and trademark ownership.

ICM is the latest company to stake out territory in the fast-growing registry landscape. The most established player in the field is Verisign, which operates both the .com and .net domains. Another outfit, Afilias, owns .info and .mobi for sites designed for mobile devices. The number of registry companies is expected to explode next year, when ICANN will allow any company to apply for its own domain extension, like .apple or .facebook.

Most big companies own tens of thousands of domain names, according to Frederick Felman, the chief marketing officer of MarkMonitor which helps companies protect their brands online. Warner Bros., for example, owns not only Warnerbros.com but also Batman.com, Harrypotter.com and Looneytunes.com among many others.

Here Come the Typosquatters

Each new domain brings a new round of cybersquatters, who register well-known trademarks to increase Web traffic or later sell them at an inflated price. Close behind are typosquatters, who register famous names with slight typographic errors, like Peppsi instead of Pepsi. The threat of rampant brand hijacking has alarmed companies who worry about the costs of defensive registrations with the launch of new domains.

A trademark owner that falls victim to cybersquatting or typosquatting must take legal action against the domain-name holder, invoking ICANN's dispute resolution policy to wrestle back the address. The process can take months and several thousand dollars in legal fees.

When ICANN opens the gates to new domains starting in January 2012, the cost of brand protection is going to skyrocket. "Multiply .xxx times several hundred, and that's the scale of the problem," said Felman.

The businesses most affected by the launch of the .xxx domain are big name adult entertainment companies, such as Canadian-based Manwin and U.S.-based Hustler, which own dozens of domain names. They are not only refusing to pay, but also demanding that ICM block their domains free of charge.

Manwin, one of the world's largest online porn companies, owns domains including Brazzers.com, XTube.com and YouPorn.com. In June, its lawyers sent a letter to Lawley, listing 57 of its preexisting domain names and warning ICM to protect those names or risk the consequences.

Manwin "has placed ICM on notice that registration of its domain names without its consent will constitute a violation of Manwin's rights," the company said in a statement. Hustler, which owns domains including Hustlertv.com, Hustlercloth ing.com and Hustlerstore.com, has sent a similar letter.

ICM responded to the legal threats with a seven-page report in July, claiming that a registry cannot be sued for trademark infringement. The letters, though, have placed ICM on notice, which increases the potential for liability if ICM sells the trademarked names, said Rosette.

No to Spongebob.xxx

Eighty percent of registrants so far have been from outside the pornography industry, according to Easyspace, a British registrar which has been taking preorders on behalf of businesses that want to protect their brands before the official registration period opens in September.

MTV Networks was among the early brands to sign up to protect names such as VH1 and Comedy Central. "This is a unique launch," said MTV spokesman Mark Jafar in an e-mailed statement. While the company will not operate a website at Spongebob.xxx, it will "be preventing others from owning it," Jafar said, noting that MTV is registering more brands with .xxx than it normally would for a new domain.

Budget Travel cited similar concerns about a potential budgettravel.xxx. If people are Googling "budget travel" while planning a vacation, "We don't want them coming across something inappropriate," said Lisa Schneider, the digital general manager for the travel site Budget Travel.

Not all registrants have to pay the $200 to $300 fee. Under ICANN's rules, certain nonprofits including the Red Cross and the International Olympic Committee receive special protection in new domains because of their international status. At ICM's request, Red Cross has submitted a list of its brand names, along with their Spanish and French translations, which will be blocked from .xxx free of charge, according to a Red Cross spokeswoman.

People for the Ethical Treatment of Animals [PETA] also signed up. However, instead of blocking its name, said PETA spokeswoman Lindsay Rajt, the organization will launch Peta.xxx as a pornography site that draws attention to the plight of animals.

"Whatever the merits and flaws of the .xxx domain, a .kids domain would be a far more useful tool for parents—and one neither Christian groups nor the porn industry should oppose."

There Should Be an Exclusively Kid-Safe Internet Domain

Jonah Goldberg and Nick Schulz

Jonah Goldberg is a contributing editor to the conservative Na-tional Review magazine. Nick Schulz is a fellow at the American Enterprise Institute for Public Policy Research, a nonpartisan conservative think tank, and the editor of its journal, the Ameri-can. In the following viewpoint, the authors argue that the best response to Internet pornography is not censorship, nor the hope-less attempt to cordon off adult content within its own .xxx top-level domain (TLD). Instead, they suggest creating a kids-only, top-level domain restricted to kid-friendly material. This plan, the authors assert, would remove the burden of attempting to monitor and restrict content on the chaotic Internet and would likely be embraced by both parents and businesses.

As you read, consider the following questions:

1. According to the authors, why is it so difficult to control access to content on the Internet?

2. Why do the authors believe that many mainstream businesses will quickly adopt and cater to the restrictions inherent in the .kids top-level domain?

3. The authors concede that creating a .kids TLD will not, by itself, make the Internet any safer for children. How would the private sector need to respond to make this proposal work?

A cross the country, schools are removing vending machines that contain sugary sodas on the grounds that kids should be kept clear of anything that might contribute to the obesity epidemic. The first lady [Michelle Obama] has made reforming school-lunch programs a high priority so that kids will consume only nutritious, healthy fare. Schools are already "drug-free zones" and "gun-free zones"—at least officially— and they have "zero tolerance" for all sorts of things. Sometimes this impulse to protect children can go too far, lending to a stultifying climate of political correctness. But nobody on the mainstream left or right disagrees with the principle that schools should be safe havens for children. And kids should be safe not just from violence, drugs, pornography, and sex predators, we agree, but also from more mundane threats, such as profanity and political indoctrination.

The Difficulty of Monitoring and Restricting Content

After school, when *in loco parentis* [in place of a parent] ends and actual parenting resumes, the same principles apply. Not all parents can live in safe and decent neighborhoods, but all good parents would if they could. None like the idea of their children turning a corner into a bad or dangerous situation in which they could be abused, exploited, or exposed to malignant influences.

Now consider the Internet. On the Internet there are no good neighborhoods and bad neighborhoods. The Web is like one vast expanse with no zoning of any kind. Nice homes sit next to crack houses, and porn theaters operate adjacent to playgrounds. The "distance" between websites is somewhere between nonexistent and trivial; indeed, the very concept of distance is inapplicable. For years, WhiteHouse.gov, the president's website, was just three letters away from White-House.com, a porn site. (The owner eventually closed down the site out of regard for his kindergartner son.) YouPorn, often called "the YouTube of porn," is a mere four letters away from YouTube. And there's hardly a bouncer at the door: The only thing separating a ten-year-old from YouPorn is a disclaimer telling visitors they must be over 18.

But even on YouTube things are not so safe for children. For example, one of the more infuriating gags is to re-dub the voice tracks on clips from children's cartoons. A friend of the authors' once let his very young daughter watch a YouTube clip of Thomas the Tank Engine while he worked at his desk nearby. He had to shut the computer off when one of the characters brought up oral sex. On another occasion, one of the authors tried to play a YouTube clip of the opening song from the old 1980s *Transformers* cartoon, only to have to pretend there was a technical problem when the profanity started to fly. Even browsing the undoctored content on YouTube, a child is merely a click or two away from something offensive or otherwise ill-suited for kids. Some libertarians say that parents should simply monitor how their children use the Web, but this argument falls short. Asking parents to look over their kids' shoulders is unrealistic. Moreover, kids should be allowed to indulge their sense of discovery. Good parents don't have to shadow their kids in the children's section of the bookstore or library.

A Network Chaotic by Design

The point isn't to pick on YouTube, which has much to recommend it. The point is rather that the Internet is a chaotic place. Part of this is by design. The "network of networks" was made to be as resilient as possible—Armageddon-proof. If one avenue of communication flow were blocked, because a nuclear bomb took out some infrastructure, or even because of mundane data-traffic bottlenecks, information would still flow freely through other avenues and get to end users. This emphasis on resilience ensured that the flow of data would be tough to control, and so the Internet would be a relatively wild and freewheeling space.

Indeed, the culture of the Internet is to oppose anything approaching actual culture. Strong cultures edit and constrict. If they did not, they wouldn't be distinct. The spirit of the Internet is to defy efforts to edit and constrict; "anything goes" is the only standard. And that's the way many people like it. Self-described Internet activists insist the Web must keep its "frontier" flavor. They reject "corporate" models of organization. Their fears have a long pedigree (long by Internet standards, at least). [Activist] Noam Chomsky was fretting about "corporate control" of the Internet back in 1998. And there is a sizable cottage industry of activist and public-interest groups, such as Free Press and Public Knowledge, that are dedicated to keeping the Internet as "open" as possible.

In this way, the activists have transformed a sensible design principle into something approaching ideology. But conservatives should be very reluctant to challenge this ethos head-on—in part because the cyber-anarchists have a point. There's something to be said for keeping the Internet out of the hands of progressive planners. [Barack] Obama adviser and former University of Chicago law professor Cass Sunstein has all sorts of elaborate ideas on how to "manage" the Internet, including mandates to ensure that Internet users are exposed to various political viewpoints. There's little reason for conservatives to cover his right flank.

And while some reasonable restraints on content and stricter safeguards for children might be warranted on the merits, there's the political calculation to consider. Beyond the usual consensus over child pornography (a consensus that, interestingly, frays at the academic, criminal, and "artistic" extremes), Americans don't like the idea of the government's censoring the Internet. They may not go as far as the Internet activists, but they go far enough that the activists can turn any intrusion by the government into a censorship controversy. And in America, censors lose censorship controversies.

Freedom from Porn

That is why any attempt to reform the way the Internet works has to be cast as a form of addition, of value-adding, of giving people more choices. This is the secret behind Apple's iPhone and iPad products. As the *Wall Street Journal*'s Eric Felten recently recounted, the Internet's frontier-culture voluptuaries despise Apple CEO Steve Jobs's App Store approach precisely because it creates safe neighborhoods (or any neighborhoods at all). By reserving the right to decide what third-party programs can be sold or used on their platforms, Apple has introduced a kind of zoning to the Internet. Ryan Tate, a tech blogger, wrote in a now-famous e-mail exchange with Jobs: "If [Bob] Dylan was 20 today, how would he feel about your company? Would he think the iPad had the faintest thing to do with 'revolution?' [sic] Revolutions are about freedom."

As Felten notes, this betrays a rather laughable misunderstanding of the history of revolutions (the Bolsheviks and Red Chinese were hardly about letting your freak flag fly). But it also reflects a less absurd and more honest disagreement over what the Internet should be about. Hence Jobs's reply: "Yep, freedom from programs that steal your private data. Freedom from programs that trash your battery." And finally: "Freedom from porn. Yep, freedom. The times they are a changin'."

Tate was horrified. "I don't want 'freedom from porn,'" he complained. "Porn is just fine!"

To which Jobs replied, "You might care more about porn when you have kids. . . ."

Tate loses this argument rather handily for the simple reason that nobody is being denied access to porn. The Apple model instead creates what might be thought of as gated communities that do not take the freewheeling climate of the Internet as their standard. You can still browse for porn if you want, but you have to leave the neighborhood, as it were, and browse on over to the red-light district.

A Modest Proposal

And this suggests what maybe the most productive way for conservatives to think about the coming Web wars. Rather than fueling the public perception that they are Comstocks [referring to anti-obscenity laws] vainly fighting for restrictions voters won't support, they should encourage government policies that permit business-model experimentation—be it the Apple model or others not yet thought of—to satisfy the desires of consumers in general and families in particular.

Here is one proposal. Right now, there are many "top-level domains"—.com, .org, .biz, .gov, .edu, etc. We propose the creation of a .kids domain that would be strictly reserved for material appropriate for minors 18 years and under. Most sites would probably be able to mirror themselves on a .kids domain with little to no extra effort. Most corporations, schools, and other organizations have perfectly harmless material that kids and teens can view without causing their parents to stay up at night. The sites of the Smithsonian, McDonald's, Disney, PBS, and countless other institutions are already perfectly safe for minors. Other websites would need a little tweaking, but not much. Only a relative handful of them—porn, dating ser-

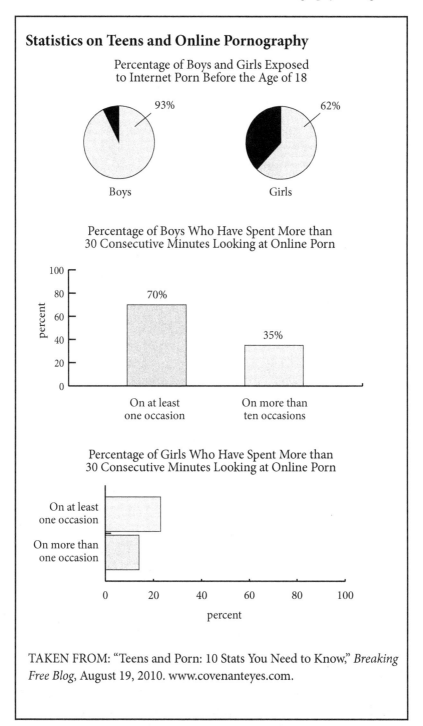

Statistics on Teens and Online Pornography

Percentage of Boys and Girls Exposed
to Internet Porn Before the Age of 18

93% — Boys

62% — Girls

Percentage of Boys Who Have Spent More than
30 Consecutive Minutes Looking at Online Porn

70% — On at least one occasion

35% — On more than ten occasions

Percentage of Girls Who Have Spent More than
30 Consecutive Minutes Looking at Online Porn

On at least one occasion

On more than one occasion

TAKEN FROM: "Teens and Porn: 10 Stats You Need to Know," *Breaking Free Blog*, August 19, 2010. www.covenanteyes.com.

vices, adult-themed chat rooms, R-rated movie sites, et al.—
would be explicitly barred from the .kids domain. The others
would simply have to tone down or pare down their offerings.

Ironically a partial model for a kids domain can be found
in .xxx domain recently approved by the international body
governing domain names (ICANN [Internet Corporation for
Assigned Names and Numbers]). A strange alliance has formed
between some porn and Christian-conservative groups. The
former don't like the new domain name because they fear it
will encourage censorship down the road; the latter oppose it
because it is voluntary, which means that porn sites can still
exist in the .com universe, and because it will further legitimize porn.

Whatever the merits and flaws of the .xxx domain, a .kids
domain would be a far more useful tool for parents—and one
neither Christian groups nor the porn industry should oppose. Social conservatives recognize the importance of providing wholesome environments for children, while porn providers insist that they have no interest in hawking their wares to
minors.

Not a Solution, but a Good Start

And our hunch is that mainstream businesses would welcome
a .kids domain. The free market is already responding to the
faults and limitations of the Internet's Wild West character:
Apple has enjoyed its brilliant success in part because it has
addressed the desires of customers (who value ease of use and
grace of design) ahead of others less attuned to consumer demand. Jobs clearly sees a wave coming—broad demand for intelligent content filters to help impose some commonsensical
order on the chaos—and he plans to ride it.

Merely creating a new domain wouldn't create a neighborhood or safe zone for kids. But it would give the private sector
the wherewithal to help parents, without handing jurisdiction
of content over to the government or requiring parents to rely

on notoriously unreliable filters. Programming a browser to recognize only a .kids address would be simple. Devices and software could be designed to make it impossible for kids to wander into bad neighborhoods.

More, Not Fewer, Options

For good or ill, the days when the consumer had to schlep down to a theater, video store, or newsstand to buy porn are over. But the red-light district was never on Main Street next to the ice-cream parlors and the family movie theater. All we are proposing is to increase the distance between the edgier and seamier aspects of the Internet and the mainstream parts. With a .kids domain, the Wild West of the Internet would still be there, but people who didn't want to let their children experience it wouldn't have to (even pioneers didn't let their small children wander too far from the homestead). Nothing would be taken away; new options would merely be created.

Any attempt to make such reforms a class issue should be resisted. As with everything involving technology, the wealthy will be early adopters of innovation. This is welcome, because without early adopters, prices don't fall and technologies don't advance. Yet the innovation we propose is remarkably "progressive," in that it would bring greater benefit to families lower on the income ladder: Working and single parents have fewer opportunities to monitor their children's activities.

This is not a sweeping argument for imposing our vision—or any vision—on the Internet. Rather, it is a modest call to facilitate the emergence of a richer Internet culture by allowing the vast majority of its users to vote with their mice, and the market to respond accordingly. Cyberspace is a big place, with plenty of room for the Wild West saloon *and* the gated community—and plenty of stuff in between.

Periodical and Internet Sources Bibliography

The following articles have been selected to supplement the diverse views presented in this chapter.

Federica Casarosa	"Protection of Minors Online: Available Regulatory Approaches," *Journal of Internet Law*, March 2011.
Neil Gaiman	"Why Defend Freedom of Icky Speech?," *Neil Gaiman Journal* (blog), December 1, 2008. http://journal.neilgaiman.com.
Joseph Galante	"The Man Who Would Be the Dot-XXX King," *BusinessWeek*, July 1, 2010.
David Gewirtz	"Should the Internet Have a .XXX TLD for Porn?," ZDNet, May 11, 2010. www.zdnet.com.
Luke Gilkerson	"The .XXX Domain: Online 'Porn Ghetto' Soon to Open for Business," *Breaking Free Blog*, October 2010. www.covenanteyes.com.
M.E. Kabay	"The Battle for Internet Freedom: Obscenity and Child Pornography," *Network World*, March 24, 2010.
Claire Perry	"Comment: We Need to Better Protect Children from Internet Porn," Politics.co.uk, November 25, 2010. www.politics.co.uk.
Dan Sabbagh	"Blocking Internet Pornography . . . That's Censorship, Isn't It?," *Organ Grinder Blog*, December 20, 2010. www.guardian.co.uk /technology/organgrinder.
Tech and Law	"Online Porn—Economics, Security, Cybercrime," May 6, 2010. http://blog .tech-and-law.com.
Carolyn Thompson	"N.Y. Case Underscores Wi-Fi Privacy Dangers," *USA Today*, April 25, 2011.

For Further Discussion

Chapter 1

1. Both pornographers and those opposed to pornography often claim that porn is a $10 to $14 billion per year industry—making it one of the largest industries in the United States. Some researchers and reporters including Susannah Breslin argue that this number is grossly inflated, and that it is unlikely that the entire worldwide porn industry accounts for even 10 percent of that claim. Why would those working within the pornography industry such as performers, producers, or distributors want to inflate the apparent impact of their industry on the US economy? Why would opponents of pornography want to do likewise?

2. It has long been claimed that exposure to sexual material—from simple depictions of nude human forms to graphic material of criminal sexual acts—is inherently damaging to children and "primes" adults to commit violent sex crimes. Although there are many anecdotes supporting this, including serial killer Ted Bundy's description of his childhood experiences with pornography, to what degree does reliable research seem to support the claim that pornography alone can drive an otherwise healthy adult to hurt others or themselves? What have researchers found? Use text from the viewpoints to support your answer.

3. An anonymous writer for the *National Review Online* documents that pornography damages personal and family relationships. Meanwhile cultural commentators like Aleks Krotoski offer examples of pornography enriching human relationships. Do you believe that pornography is

generally beneficial or damaging to human relationships, or is there something else going on that has little or nothing to do with pornography itself? Explain your reasoning.

Chapter 2

1. Is pornography addictive? If so, what is meant by "addiction," and is that different than addiction to cocaine or methamphetamine? If not, then why is it that far more people seem to develop an unhealthy, compulsive need for pornography than develop similar obsessions with other "naturally" pleasurable and exciting experiences like riding roller coasters, dancing at parties, or drinking milkshakes?

2. Is sexting a normal part of an adolescent's sexual coming-of-age, or a dangerous mistake—especially for girls? Are girls punished disproportionately both legally and socially for expressing their sexuality in this way? Are they correspondingly in some situations disproportionately rewarded for expressing their sexuality online, as Benjamin Wallace seems to imply? Why?

Chapter 3

1. Does simply seeing Internet pornography warp sexual development in teens? In what ways might it impact self-image and sexual expectations? Do you see both negative and positive impacts? If you believe that online pornography *does* affect teen self-image and sexual expectations, are these effects unique to pornography, or do other parts of the media landscape—movies, television advertisements, magazines, reality programming—contribute to these ideas?

2. Is pornography especially damaging to boys? Summarize Marnia Robinson's and Christopher Shulgan's arguments, and indicate which you believe is more convincing, and why.

3. According to Milton Diamond, Eva Jozifkova, and Petr Weiss, there seems to be a correlation between the increased availability of child pornography and a decrease in sex crimes committed against children. Is this surprising? What policy decisions might one suggest based on this information? Would any politician ever say such things publicly? Explain.

Chapter 4

1. Can online pornography be regulated? What obstacles exist to regulating online pornography, and how might these be overcome? Should online pornography be regulated? Why or why not? What risks are posed by such regulations? Based on everything you've seen in the preceding chapters, are there real and urgent reasons to regulate Internet pornography? What are these?

2. Nick Clark argues that all pornography should be restricted to the .xxx top-level Internet domain (i.e., all pornographic websites would have a name ending in ".xxx" instead of ".com" or anything else) to protect children from being exposed to pornography, and to limit the spread of child pornography. Meanwhile, political commentators like Jonah Goldberg and Nick Schulz argue that it makes more sense to create a verifiably porn-free "walled garden" through a ".kids" domain that *only* includes kid-friendly material, rather than attempt to herd all pornography into .xxx domains. Which plan seems most workable to you, technologically, socially, and politically? Who stands to profit from these changes, and how?

Organizations to Contact

The editors have compiled the following list of organizations concerned with the issues debated in this book. The descriptions are derived from materials provided by the organizations. All have publications or information available for interested readers. The list was compiled on the date of publication of the present volume; the information provided here may change. Be aware that many organizations take several weeks or longer to respond to inquiries, so allow as much time as possible.

Adult Freedom Foundation (AFF)
119 E. Montgomery Avenue, Suite 2, Ardmore, PA   19003
(610) 896-5558
website: www.adultfreedomfoundation.org

The Adult Freedom Foundation (AFF) is a watchdog group for the adult entertainment industry that works to protect First Amendment rights and dispel myths about pornography and its impact on individuals and society. The group works to connect members of the mainstream media and government to legal, scientific, and industry experts. Its website archives news pertaining to free speech and the adult entertainment industry.

American Civil Liberties Union (ACLU)
125 Broad Street, 18th Floor, New York, NY   10004
(212) 549-2500
e-mail: aclu@aclu.org
website: www.aclu.org

The American Civil Liberties Union (ACLU) is dedicated to preserving freedoms of expression and religious practice, as well as rights to privacy, due process, and equal protection under the law. The ACLU provides free legal services to those whose rights have been violated. The ACLU website offers an array of policy statements, pamphlets, and fact sheets on civil rights issues, including "Network Neutrality 101—Why the Government Must Act to Preserve the Free and Open Internet" and "We Must Combat Child Pornography Without Abandoning Online Privacy."

Association of Sites Advocating Child Protection (ASACP)

5042 Wilshire Boulevard, #540, Los Angeles, CA 90036-4305
(323) 908-7864
website: www.asacp.org

The Association of Sites Advocating Child Protection (ASACP) is a nonprofit organization dedicated to eliminating child pornography from the Internet. ASACP is almost exclusively funded by sponsors from the online adult entertainment industry. All ASACP member companies are required to comply with the group's code of ethics. The ASACP website includes statistics on online child pornography as well as resources geared toward parents and adult website operators.

Family Research Council (FRC)

801 G Street NW, Washington, DC 20001
1-800-225-4008
website: www.frc.org

The Family Research Council (FRC) is a Washington, DC-based nonprofit organization that seeks to promote "faith, family and freedom in public policy and public opinion." The FRC largely focuses on the rights of traditional families, parental rights, the right to life, and the protection of children from inappropriate images in the media. Its website includes articles, press releases, opinion pieces, news, and position papers, such as "From Playboy to Pedophilia: How Adult Sexual Liberation Leads to Children's Sexual Exploitation."

Focus on the Family

8605 Explorer Drive, Colorado Springs, CO 80920
1-800-232-6459
website: www.focusonthefamily.com

Focus on the Family describes itself as a "global Christian ministry dedicated to helping families thrive." It provides help and resources for couples looking to build stable marriages and families in accordance with Christian values, and to raise children according to "morals and values grounded in biblical principles." The Focus on the Family website includes many resources for Christian families, including a series of articles addressing "Pornography and Virtual Infidelity" and "When Children View Pornography."

Free Speech Coalition (FSC)

PO Box 10480, Canoga Park, CA 91309
(818) 348-9373
e-mail: info@freespeechcoalition.com
website: www.freespeechcoalition.com

The Free Speech Coalition (FSC) is a trade association for the adult entertainment industry. Its mission includes publicly advocating for the adult entertainment industry, guarding against unconstitutional government intervention into the industry, and advising its members on good business practices. Its publications include the weekly industry newsletter *X-Press*, as well as an annual state-of-the-industry report, white papers on topics like pornography addiction, and health and ethics manuals for adult entertainment businesses.

National Center for Missing and Exploited Children (NCMEC)

Charles B. Wang International Children's Building
699 Prince Street, Alexandria, VA 22314-3175
(703) 224-2150
website: www.missingkids.com

The National Center for Missing and Exploited Children (NCMEC) is a private, nonprofit organization established by the US Congress in 1984. NCMEC serves as the nation's primary informational resource concerning missing and sexually exploited children. The organization provides information and resources to law enforcement, other professionals, parents, and children. Its website includes many articles and reports on child pornography and online exploitation.

Pink Cross Foundation

6077 Coffee Road #4, PMB 33, Bakersfield, CA   93308
e-mail: info@thepinkcross.org
website: www.thepinkcross.org

The Pink Cross Foundation is a faith-based, nonprofit humanitarian education and outreach organization serving sex workers looking to exit the adult entertainment industry. The Pink Cross Foundation also reaches out to offer support to those struggling with pornography in their communities or personal lives. It supports legislation to enforce health and safety regulations within the porn industry. Its website includes news, information, statistics, and extensive interviews with former adult entertainers and sex workers.

XXX Church

PO Box 50048, Pasadena, CA   91115
(626) 628-3387
e-mail: info@xxxchurch.com
website: www.xxxchurch.com

XXX Church is a nonprofit Christian organization aiming to help those who struggle with pornography, including both consumers and performers. The group describes itself as "the #1 Christian porn site designed to bring awareness, openness and accountability to those affected by pornography." Its website includes blog posts, videos, articles, and other resources tailored to men, women, teens, parents, and those within the adult entertainment industry.

Bibliography of Books

| Feona Attwood, ed. | *Mainstreaming Sex: The Sexualization of Western Culture.* New York: I.B. Tauris, 2009. |

| Feona Attwood, ed. | *Porn.com: Making Sense of Online Pornography.* New York: Peter Lang, 2010. |

| Mardia J. Bishop and Ann C. Hall, eds. | *Pop-Porn: Pornography in American Culture.* Westport, CT: Praeger, 2007. |

| Gail Dines | *Pornland: How Porn Has Hijacked Our Sexuality.* Boston: Beacon Press, 2010. |

| M. Gigi Durham | *The Lolita Effect: The Media Sexualization of Young Girls and What We Can Do About It.* Woodstock, NY: Overlook Press, 2008. |

| Andrea Dworkin | *Pornography: Men Possessing Women.* New York: Putnam, 1981. |

| Donna M. Hughes and James R. Stoner Jr., eds. | *The Social Costs of Pornography: A Collection of Papers.* Princeton, NJ: Witherspoon Institute, 2010. |

| Philip Jenkins | *Beyond Tolerance: Child Pornography on the Internet.* New York: New York University Press, 2001. |

Michael Kimmel — *Guyland: The Perilous World Where Boys Become Men.* New York: Harper, 2008.

Frederick S. Lane III — *Obscene Profits: The Entrepreneurs of Pornography in the Cyber Age.* New York: Routledge Books, 2000.

Michael Leahy — *Porn Nation: Conquering America's #1 Addiction.* Chicago: Northfield Publishing, 2008.

Judith Levine — *Harmful to Minors: The Perils of Protecting Children from Sex.* Minneapolis: University of Minnesota Press, 2002.

Ariel Levy — *Female Chauvinist Pigs: Women and the Rise of Raunch Culture.* New York: Free Press, 2006.

Wendy Maltz and Larry Maltz — *The Porn Trap: The Essential Guide to Overcoming Problems Caused by Pornography.* New York: HarperCollins, 2008.

Joe S. McIlhaney and Freda McKissic Bush — *Hooked: New Science on How Casual Sex Is Affecting Our Children.* Chicago: Northfield Publishing, 2008.

Alan McKee, Katherine Albury, and Catherine Lumby — *The Porn Report.* Carlton, Victoria: Melbourne University Publishing, 2008.

Brian McNair — *Striptease Culture: Sex, Media and Democratization of Desire.* New York: Routledge, 2002.

Pamela Paul	*Pornified: How Pornography Is Transforming Our Lives, Our Relationships, and Our Families.* New York: Times Books, 2005.
Audacia Ray	*Naked on the Internet: Hookups, Downloads, and Cashing in on Internet Sexploration.* Emeryville, CA: Seal Press, 2007.
Marnia Robinson	*Cupid's Poisoned Arrow: From Habit to Harmony in Sexual Relationships.* Berkeley, CA: North Atlantic Books, 2009.
Carmine Sarracino and Kevin M. Scott	*The Porning of America: The Rise of Porn Culture, What It Means, and Where We Go from Here.* Boston: Beacon Press, 2008.
Eric Schlosser	*Reefer Madness: Sex, Drugs, and Cheap Labor in the American Black Market.* Boston: Houghton Mifflin, 2004.
Nadine Strossen	*Defending Pornography: Free Speech, Sex, and the Fight for Women's Rights.* New York: New York University Press, 2000.
William M. Struthers	*Wired for Intimacy: How Pornography Hijacks the Male Brain.* Downers Grove, IL: IVP Books, 2009.
Jessica Valenti	*Full Frontal Feminism: A Young Woman's Guide to Why Feminism Matters.* Emeryville, CA: Seal Press, 2007.

Index

CPSIA information can be obtained
at www.ICGtesting.com
Printed in the USA
FSHW04n1930150418
46914FS